POINT OF OPINION

Adventures in Parliamentary Simplicity

By H. W. Farwell,
Certified Professional Parliamentarian

Copyright © 2004 by H.W. Farwell

ISBN 0-7414-2335-9

Published by:

INFI∞ITY
PUBLISHING.COM

1094 New De Haven Street, Suite 100
West Conshohocken, PA 19428-2713
Info@buybooksontheweb.com
www.buybooksontheweb.com
Toll-free (877) BUY BOOK
Local Phone (610) 941-9999
Fax (610) 941-9959

∞

Printed in the United States of America

Printed on Recycled Paper

Published January 2005

Dedicated to

FLOYD M. RIDDICK

Parliamentarian, Teacher, Mentor and Inspiration

I dared to express many of these ideas because of his
support, his encouragement, and
his friendship.

Also by H. W. Farwell

THE MAJORITY RULES:
A Manual of Procedure for MOST Groups

and handy pocketbooks of parliamentary details

PARLIAMENTARY MOTIONS
(for Sturgis Standard Rules)

MAJORITY MOTIONS
(for Farwell's Majority Rules)

CONTENTS

PREFACE

A "Point of Order" is a parliamentary device to call attention to the proper use of complex rules. This book, "Point of Opinion," is a device to call attention to opinions about those rules.

Parliamentary procedure is a highly effective tool for group decision-making. Many people have managed to stay clear of it, dismissing it as complicated, unnecessary, troublesome, and useful only as a method for keeping people from having what they want. Sometimes it is just a procedure used to allow some people to show off and enhance their egos.

Parliamentary procedure is complicated. Parliamentary procedure can be difficult. It does not have to be troublesome. It can be an orderly and fair method to authorize or defeat some proposal. I believe that parliamentary procedure is a safeguard of the rights of every member of an organization. Such an organization may be small and informal, large and meticulously formal, or even national in scope. Nevertheless, parliamentary procedure permits every member of a group to voice opinions and to participate in making final decisions that can affect organizational operation.

As such, parliamentary procedure is an essential element of democracy and, consequently, should be understood and used by every caring citizen of this country.

Although this nation started out as a democracy where every member of the population participated in government, a practice now found only in old-fashioned New England town meetings and certain Quaker congregations, we became a democratic republic. According to our Constitution, we are not directly concerned in governing the nation: we elect others to be our representatives at national legislative assemblies. This is a fortunate arrangement, for if all of the many millions of our population had to assemble, discuss, and then vote on every national issue, we could never progress.

Electing legislators in a democratic republic requires that certain rules must be established so that every citizen can be fairly and equally represented. That is the role of parliamentary procedure and is the reason why everyone should understand it and be able to use it.

Unfortunately, not every citizen can understand it. Only a very few citizens can use it correctly.

We teach rules of mathematics, rules of grammar, even rules of various sports in our schools, but we have greatly neglected the rules of orderly decision-making. The reason for this is simple – we have invested parliamentary procedure with such mysterious complexity and intimidating language that the uninitiated approach with fear and trembling, if they come near it at all.

This book presents a very personal point of view that, I hope, will convince readers that there is no mystery in parliamentary procedure. It is comprised of articles written and published during the past forty years. Some are vaguely technical, some are vaguely humorous, and all of them are designed to demonstrate a great truth.

Good parliamentary procedure is the application of simple courtesy, simple tact, and simple common sense to group decision making.

FOREWORD

The term "parliamentary law" does not refer to a piece of legislation. You won't find it in the United States Constitution, not even among the amendments. The most famous American writer to produce a little guidebook on the subject, Henry Robert, was not an attorney at all but an army engineer. Over the years, his book has grown to resemble an encyclopedia, but his intent was coordination, not legislation. He thought any American moving from the Midwest to the Pacific Coast should be able to participate fully in the civic, social, or religious groups of his choice, since the procedures for official group action should be the same in all locations.

If these groups were to be democratic, an obvious requirement would be effective communication. Individuals must be able to share ideas, understand each other, persuade one another, until the best thinking of individuals becomes the policy of the group. Formal procedures should facilitate such communication.

Unfortunately, the "Robert's Rules" of today has become a library of obscure regulations to settle rare points of conflict. Such a resource, highly complex and often little understood, is of limited use in guiding the deliberations of the average democratic groups in which most of us are involved. For us, writers like Professor Farwell provide the needed help. He has been active in such organizations as the American Institute of Parliamentarians, the National Association of Parliamentarians, and the Commission on American Parliamentary Practice, even holding office and editing a journal. But he speaks and writes as a specialist in communication, not as an attorney.

Now "Hy" Farwell has assembled the best of his thinking and writing on democratic procedure for the last forty years, in his new book, POINT OF OPINION. We can certainly agree with him that if the rules of football were "as complicated as those of parliamentary procedure, the game might never be played." Here, this professor of communication shares his thinking about simplifying, clarifying, and making effective the procedures governing most democratic groups, the theory behind his earlier *MAJORITY RULES* manual.

We are grateful that he shares these insights, and every parliamentarian must give respectful attention as he raises his "Point of Opinion."

John E. Baird, Ph.D

John Baird is a director of the AIP-Hearst National Parliamentary Education Project for Colleges and Universities, and prior to his retirement, was Professor of Speech Communication at California State Universitry - Hayward,

ACKNOWLEDGEMENTS

I recognise with enormous gratitude the debt I owe to my wife, Martha, for her proofreading skill, her sorely-tried patience and her continual encouragement during many years; to John Baird for his critical view of this work, to Edward Bliss for urging me on, and almost more than any other, to my grandson, Kevin D. Farwell, for his extraordinary technical computer skill, without which the text of this book would have been frozen forever on several reams of paper in my study

H. W. Farwell
Pueblo, Colorado

.

A NEW QUORUM REQUIREMENT

George Walters was disgusted. He came home from the school board meeting and flung his hat into the big chair beside the closet door. Katherine was amazed for George had always hung his hat carefully in the closet. He was meticulous in both dress and conduct.

"George, whatever is wrong?"

George snorted, "Mrs. Kaufman moved to have our school board meetings in the afternoon, instead of in the evening – and she wants to serve tea! And the worst part was that I couldn't do anything about it!"

Katherine frowned, for she knew that George was proud of his parliamentary skill. Surely he could easily handle this ridiculous proposal.

George continued, "Then Cora Weber seconded the motion. Everyone was laughing so much at the idea that when Chairman Smith called for the vote, everyone simply sat there. Three women voted for the stupid motion and no one voted against it. So the motion passed and we just ignored the whole thing. Later, when only six of us were still there, the chairman reminded us that our next meeting would be at three o'clock next Tuesday and that tea would be served. I told him that it was silly to have an afternoon meeting, especially with tea, but he said we had made a definite decision. Well, I moved to reconsider, but a couple of fellows had gone home and we no longer had a quorum present.

There was nothing we could do. We had to agree to have the early meeting."

Katherine thought for a minute. "But with only three people voting to have afternoon meetings – that couldn't be legal, could it? After all, you have fifteen people on the board. Don't you have to have a quorum present?"

"Yes," said George, "we have fifteen members on the board and a quorum of eight must be present to have a legal meeting. The problem lies in the fact that a quorum was present – there were at least thirteen of us in the room when that crazy Mrs. Kaufman made her motion. But most of us figured it was a joke so we didn't vote. We were present but we abstained."

"And so the motion passed? The whole board has to meet in the afternoon?"

George was disgusted. "Yeah! There ought to be some kind of rule so that things like this couldn't happen."

BUT IT DID HAPPEN. And it may happen again!

-oOo-

For situations such as this, a new rule should be established. I propose the following:

The vote on a motion is not valid unless the number of participating voters, both those in favor and those against the motion, is equal to or greater than a majority of the quorum of the assembly.

There is a good argument in favor of such a requirement. Most importantly, it protects the members of an organization from hasty decisions made by just a few people at a time when, due to apathy or lack of understanding, a large number of potential voters abstain. The existing requirement for a quorum protects those members who are absent from decisions made when only a small number has attended a meeting. The proposed new rule would protect those members who are actually present but, for one reason or another, are unaware of the details or implications of the pending question.

The traditional rule insists that no meeting is legal unless a quorum is present, but also tells us that once it is established, the presence of a full quorum is "presumed", unless it is questioned. Thus it is perfectly possible and proper for a lengthy meeting which required the presence of a quorum of ten to function, to make decisions even after all but five people have departed.

A second benefit of this requirement would be that members would be motivated to participate in the activities of the meeting. Frequently, and especially at more informal meetings, purposeful assemblies deteriorate into social events and members attend with little concern for business which might be transacted.

A strong vote against this proposed rule is based upon my belief that the right to abstain must be as carefully protected as the right to vote. Not everything can be either right or wrong. Many things can be perceived only in shades of gray. When an individual is required to take sides and vote either for black or white, it may be far wiser to abstain.

-o0o-

The ultimate fate of this proposed requirement lies in the future. Possibly some recognized parliamentary authority might incorporate it into a new parliamentary code. Possibly some organization may think it would be a good rule and weaves it into its bylaws and standing rules. Other societies may observe the practice and adopt it and it spreads like ripples in a still pond.

But if no one notices it, it will, like many other possible improvements, wither on the vine and eventually disappear.[1]

THE FIRST THREE WORDS

1987! That was the year we celebrated the 200th anniversary of the signing of our national Constitution! There were no vast demonstrations, no parades of tall ships, no fireworks. Despite that, the bicentennial celebration of our Constitution commemorated an even more significant event than the signing of the Declaration of Independence. By no means do I depreciate the importance of July Fourth, 1776, but once we had gained our independence from Great Britain, we could have traveled any of several roads. But due to the courage and initiative of men like Washington, Madison, Franklin, Hamilton, and Jefferson, our national philosophy, which had been forged by the Declaration of Independence and tempered by the fire of the Revolution, was made imperishable in the words of our Constitution.

The lifespan of the Declaration of Independence began on July 4th, 1776, when a few individuals believed that we should be free and it lasted only until the defeat of Lord Cornwallis at Yorktown and the signing of the Treaty of Paris in 1783. At that time, the whole civilized world formally recognized us as a new and independent nation. A new and independent nation, however, can become almost anything. What we did become, and what we are today, is directly related to our Constitution, a vital living document which is as meaningful to us as it was to those who wrote it more than two hundred years ago

Listen to these words:.

> WE THE PEOPLE of the United States, in Order to form a more perfect Union, establish Justice, insure domestic Tranquillity, provide for the Common Defense, promote the general

Welfare, and secure the Blessings of Liberty for ourselves and our Posterity, do ordain and establish this Constitution for the United States of America.

That's how it begins. Those are the words of the Preamble of the Constitution of the United States of America, a document which has taken its place among the most significant writings of our civilization, a document created more than two hundred years ago which has enabled us to attain power, prestige and prominence, not only as a nation, but as individuals banded together by a single majestic ideal.

Almost every nation has a constitution of some sort. Some, like Great Britain, have no single, formal document, but rely upon a body of laws that have been developed over many centuries. Others, such as the now defunct Soviet Union, use a constitution patterned roughly upon democratic principles but based upon the concept of an all-powerful state controlled by a very small group such as the fourteen-member Politburo. Still other nations have constitutions not unlike our own.

Yet, of approximately two hundred nations of this world, the United States remains unique. When we ask ourselves why, there is but one simple answer. We stand apart from all other countries because of our Constitution, a document which welded together a group of thirteen fiercely independent, self-governing states into a strong and united nation. Our Constitution embodies an inspired system of checks and balances which has both regulated and protected the rights, freedoms and obligations of the executive, legislative and judicial branches of our government and of the people of this nation.

But the system of checks and balances, the establishment of a strong national government, the division of the government into three branches, the fact that it created a single chief executive officer, the fact that it is a formal written document — none of these is the key to the real significance of our Constitution. While all of these factors have undoubtedly contributed to the greatness of our country, the real magic lies in just three of its four thousand, five hundred and forty-three words — the first three words — "WE THE PEOPLE."

These three words symbolize the very essence of our country. They symbolize the starting point of our national philosophy, the foundation of governmental power and authority, the cornerstone of the United States of America.

WE THE PEOPLE — in those three words our Constitution designates the people of the United States as the source of ultimate power and authority, and with those three words, our nation took the first steps toward greatness — WE THE PEOPLE — not an all-powerful state, not a self-appointed ruler or a victorious conqueror, not even a monarch who holds power by divine right or family inheritance — none of these! The source of our governmental power is written in those first three words — WE THE PEOPLE!

Our Constitution is a document that was, indeed, conceived and developed by WE THE PEOPLE, but its birth was not a painless one. In fact, during its gestation, there were frequent times when all effort seemed in vain, for, history tells us, not everyone favored such a firm and centralized form of government.

We have all read of the chaos and confusion which existed under the Articles of Confederation, a weak agreement by which the thirteen states implemented a single-chambered Congress composed of representatives appointed by the State Assemblies. While authorizing Congress certain powers, each state retained "its sovereignty, freedom and independence and every power, jurisdiction and right." Congress could not levy taxes nor did it have the authority to enforce any of its decisions. Each State felt free to issue its own currency, to maintain its own navy, and many times neglected to send enough representatives to Philadelphia to provide a quorum. John Hancock, elected President of the Congress in 1785, took his duties so lightly that he rarely bothered to attend.

George Washington wondered whether the Revolution had been worth all the suffering and bloodshed. "We are either a united people under one head, for Federal purposes," he wrote, "or we are thirteen thousand independent sovereignties, eternally counteracting each other." The Articles of Confederation, intended to unite the states in a "firm league of friendship" were, in Washington's words, "little more than the shadow without the substance."

And so it was that in 1786, several states followed the leadership of Virginia and issued an invitation to all thirteen states to meet in Philadelphia the following May to "render the Constitution of the United States adequate to the exigencies of the Union."

Forced by this action, the Continental Congress itself then issued a call for a constitutional convention, specifically stating that it was "for the sole and express purpose of revising the Articles of Confederation and reporting to Congress and the several legislatures such alterations and provisions therein." In response, eight states instructed their delegates to operate under the Virginia call, while four limited their delegations to the revision of the Articles of Confederation as specified by the Continental Congress. Rhode Island refused to send any delegation at all.

In this brief summary of the first faltering footsteps of our nation, I have mentioned only one parliamentary aspect-- the Quorum. I stated that the Continental Congress was frequently unable to conduct business because of its inability to muster a quorum. This, however, was the result of indifference, not ignorance. Those early statesmen were not ignorant of procedure and it played an important role in their actions. They had committees, they presented resolutions, and they made motions. Our founding fathers were familiar with parliamentary procedure — they knew it, they understood it, and they used it.

Almost daily, from May 30th, 1787, to July 24th, the members of the Convention resolved themselves into a Committee of the Whole in the early part of the day and transacted all business, including much debate under committee rules, until late afternoon. Although George Washington had been elected President of the Convention on the very first day of business, Nathaniel Gorham of Massachusetts, who had just completed a term as President of the Continental Congress, was elected Chairman of the Committee of the Whole.

It took almost forty days for the Committee of the Whole to debate. Indeed, it almost came to blows over such controversial matters as the question of whether there should be a single chief executive or a committee of several; whether there should be proportional representation or should the one man/one vote formula apply; whether the chief executive should be elected by the people or by the legislators; should the term of office of the chief executive be six, eleven, or twenty years or should he serve, like the Justices of the Supreme Court, "during good behavior," the lifetime term of office as defined, even today, in our Constitution.

All in all, the Committee of the Whole adopted about thirty resolutions and considered, but did not adopt, several other plans. From July 18th to the 24th, the Committee reported its recommendations to the Convention where, of course, considerable additional debate occurred. On July 24th, however, the approved resolutions were referred to a new committee, the five-man Committee on Detail. chaired by John Rutledge of South Carolina. The Committee on Detail was given ten days to combine the referred material into a draft constitution. The Convention then recessed.

During the next ten days, the Committee on Detail struggled with their monumental task. They also considered parts of the Articles of Confederation, they discussed some of the better sections of various state constitutions and some of the features of several of the plans that had been suggested to the Committee of the Whole but not approved. Edmund Randolph, a member of the Committee, wrote that it was essential that simple and precise language be used to avoid misunderstandings, and most importantly,

> ...To insert essential principles only, lest the operations of government should be clogged by rendering those provisions permanent and unalterable which ought to be accommodated to times and events.[2]

Parliamentarians and those they serve can profit greatly from these words. When called upon to prepare bylaws for organizations or to assist in drafting proposed amendments, they should remember Randolph's instructions, "... to insert essential principles only, lest the operations of government be clogged by rendering those provisions permanent and unalterable which ought to be accommodated to times and events." They should suggest that the specific details be left to some parliamentary guide, just as our national legislatures rely upon Riddick's *Senate Rules* and Deschler's *Rules of the House of Representatives*. They should encourage those they serve to have bylaws which prescribe only the objectives of their organizations, spelling out the details of procedure by which business is transacted in Standing Rules — which may be "accommodated to times and events."

On August 6th, the Convention reconvened to consider the work of the Committee on Detail. Needless to say, extensive and exhaustive debate and discussion followed. It is interesting to note that at this time the delegates were getting anxious to finish their work and several weary members had already returned to their homes. The Convention found it appropriate to appoint a Committee on Postponed Matters to which all items still delayed by controversy and conflict were referred for the development of compromise recommendations. It was a month before consensus could be reached on matters such as the qualifications of voters, the powers of the President, the power of the Congress to issue paper money and similar matters.

Finally, however, the new Constitution was unanimously approved by all twelve states. The vote within several delegations was not unanimous, however, and a minority of members made several last-minute attempts to present additional amendments. Despite his personal dissatisfaction with several key points, Benjamin Franklin offered some words of wisdom which apply to deliberative assemblies today as much as they did to the assembled delegates at the Constitutional Convention in Philadelphia in August, 1787. In part, he said,

> Mr. President, I confess that there are several parts of this Constitution which I do not at present approve, but I am not sure that I shall never approve them. For, having lived so long, I have experienced many instances of being obliged by better information or fuller consideration to change opinions, even on important subjects, which I had once thought right but found to be otherwise. It is therefore that the older I grow, the more apt I am to doubt my own judgment and to pay more respect to the judgment of others.

> ... I doubt whether any other convention we can obtain may be able to make a better constitution. For when you assemble a number of men to have the advantage of their joint wisdom, you invariably assemble with those men all their prejudices, their passions, their errors of opinion, their local interests and their selfish views. From such an assembly, can a perfect product be expected?

It therefore astonishes me to find this system approaching so near to perfection as it does . . ..

Thus I consent, Sir, to this Constitution, because I cannot help expressing a wish that every member of this Convention who may still have objection to it would with me, on this occasion, doubt a little of his own infallibility and, to make manifest our unanimity, put his name to this document.[3]

On September 17th, 1787, the new Constitution was signed by thirty-six of the forty-one delegates present. The Constitutional Convention then adjourned *sine die.*

Let's turn our attention to those basic principles long accepted as the foundations of parliamentary practice: Freedom of Choice; Open Debate; Voluntary Decisions; Majority Rule; Minority Rights; Absentee Rights; Equality of Members; and the promotion of Order and Justice.

Freedom of Choice

By this we mean that every member may vote and has the right to do so without fear of reprisal.

Open Debate

We interpret this as the right of every person to speak and to be heard.

Voluntary Decisions

These are made by members based upon each individual's understanding of the facts and circumstances, not because of intimidation and threats.

Majority Rule

This is commonly understood to apply to decisions made when more than half a group agrees, while preserving the Minority Rights of those who disagree.

Equality of Membership

This does not permit any preferential treatment of members because of race, status or other factor, and when we consider the Rights of Absentees we are remembering that "Taxation without Representation is Tyranny!"

Order and Justice

We are concerned with the promotion of Order and Justice because without Order, we have nothing but chaos and only with Order and rules of procedure may we hope to progress. Without Justice, we cannot be fair and equal.

-o0o-

These six fundamentals are far more than the bases of parliamentary procedure-- WE THE PEOPLE have incorporated them into the very fabric of our Constitution and of our Nation.

It doesn't take much effort to find reflections of these parliamentary principles in our Constitution. And it takes even less effort to see how the philosophy of the fifty-five men who assembled in Philadelphia in the summer of 1787 has affected modern parliamentary practice. WE THE PEOPLE of the United States may exist forever shielded by our Constitution from tyranny and oppression, but we must continually guard against even minor infringements of the guarantees provided to us by our Constitution, and help others to do the same. A minor infringement, left unchecked, may become monstrous.

How easy it is to find organizations, big and small, where the power — the source of real authority — has imperceptibly shifted from WE THE PEOPLE to small groups of ambitious, self-serving leaders who permit little if any challenge to their actions. How easy it is to point to examples of misuse of authority — to petty dictatorships — to cronyism and intolerance. There are far too many cases to mention of leaders who loudly profess their willingness to fight to the death to preserve our Constitution, but who, because of ambition, ignorance, or indifference, disregard all its provisions, Federal, state and local laws or even their own bylaws because WE THE PEOPLE take too long to discuss openly and vote voluntarily to reach decisions.

I shall never forget the mayor of a small town who told me that he didn't need a parliamentarian, "I just tell them how to vote and they do it and that is all there is to it!" Any historian will remind you that both Adolph Hitler and Benito Mussolini got things done! For the first and only time in centuries, the streets of Rome were clear of beggars — the railroad trains of Germany won international acclaim for cleanliness and punctuality. WE THE PEOPLE do take longer to reach decisions because we listen to the opinions and arguments of every person who desires to speak and then we make decisions by consensus or majority vote. WE THE PEOPLE can never be as efficient as a dictator. But we must always be cautious not to relinquish, for the sake of efficiency, so much power and authority to an organization that WE THE PEOPLE can no longer control our own destiny.

When we join any organization, we voluntarily surrender a small measure of our personal, individual rights. We do this because we know that only in this way can we "promote order." We value the right to discuss matters openly and freely, but we know that were everyone to speak simultaneously, total confusion would result. It has been well said that you can listen best with your mouth closed.

If you are a member of the vast, unorganized group of automobile drivers in the United States, you have automatically agreed to sacrifice your right to drive anywhere you care to drive at any speed. By accepting your driver's license, you have agreed to drive on the right side of the road and to obey the speed limits.

You like to spend your evenings at home with your family, but you join an organization that meets on Wednesdays at 7:30 p.m. You surrender your right to be with your family because you want to share in the group's goals and achievements.

You believe that your club dues are adequate to meet expenses, but the majority of the members voted to raise the dues by 10 percent. Even though you feel that this decision is both unwise and unnecessary, you must either accept it and pay the increase, or forfeit your membership in the organization.

We recognize that we sacrifice some of our personal liberty and our individual rights for the good of the group — but woe betide us were we ever to abandon all our rights and permit the group to establish itself as the source of all power. If members were to allow an organization to become the supreme authority by usurping their rights and powers, they have changed from decision-making participants — and become slaves! If an all-powerful state can decide what's right and what is wrong based upon what is best for the State, its citizens cannot Speak Freely, they cannot enjoy Domestic Tranquillity, nor can they inherit the Blessings of Liberty for themselves and their Posterity. And, of course, in such a state there would be no need and no place for parliamentarians.

It is not easy to contemplate our Constitution without simultaneously considering its first ten amendments, the Bill of Rights. Even though it was December 15th, 1791, before the Bill of Rights was added to the Constitution, I consider it an integral element despite the fact that a national bicentennial celebration of its ratification was hardly worth a headline on the inside pages of our newspapers, and because I feel strongly that the relationship between parliamentary procedure and our Constitution was strengthened enormously by various sections of the Bill of Rights.

The First Amendment, which prohibits any abridgment of the Freedom of Speech and guarantees the right of the people "peaceably to assemble," is surely relevant. The rights of absentees; the rights of minorities; the promotion of Order and Justice; the equality of members — all of these are affected by the Fourth, Fifth, Sixth, Seventh, and Eighth Amendments.

Let's return to the Preamble of the Constitution. In one sentence, this statement sums up so much of the philosophy of the United States that WE THE PEOPLE would do well to memorize it — to engrave it on our buildings — and to teach it to the generations who will succeed us. Look at it more closely. Stripped of its explanatory clauses, this simple statement says, "WE THE PEOPLE of the United States ... do ordain and establish this Constitution. ..." That's all there is to it! WE THE PEOPLE established the Constitution! No monarch did it, no dictator did it, no invisible state did it! WE THE PEOPLE did it!

The Declaration of Independence made the American colonies independent from the British crown. The Constitution of the United States created a new and vital nation. WE THE PEOPLE are the beneficiaries of these two documents and only our eternal vigilance can preserve the legacy of freedom, strength, justice, and equality our forefathers bequeathed us. Those parliamentary principles of which I spoke provide a barricade, which can protect us as it protects the rights and privileges guaranteed by the Constitution. In the words of the late Supreme Court Justice William O. Douglas,

> Procedure is more than formality. Procedure is, indeed, the great mainstay of substantive rights. ...Without procedural safeguards, liberty would rest on precarious grounds. It is our task to in-

sure that the safeguards provided by parliamentary procedure are understood, maintained and rigidly enforced.[4]

Today, more than two hundred years after the Constitution was signed, many people take it for granted. Despite its precision and clarity, few people other than lawyers and legislators have read and understood it — if, indeed, they really read it.

Today, more than one hundred years after the publication of Henry Martyn Robert's *Pocket Manual of Rules of Order for Deliberative Assemblies*, and despite the sale of many millions of copies of the *Rules of Order*, comparatively few people, including lawyers and legislators, have read and understood the skills, the techniques, and, most of all, the philosophy of parliamentary procedure.

Today, as in 1776, as in 1788, as in 1861, as in 1941, as in September, 2001, as in almost any day of our complex, chaotic world, group decision-making plays an essential role in determining where we are going, how we will get there, and even where we are today. Parliamentary procedure is the ultimate tool of group decision-making.

Today, and in all the years to come, there is and will always be a challenge for all of us. If we genuinely desire to insure the objectives voiced by our founding fathers in 1787 — the more perfect union, domestic tranquillity, provision for the common defense, promotion of the general welfare and the blessings of liberty for ourselves and our posterity — we must always keep before us the single fundamental concept that the true source of power and authority in our nation is — and must always be — found in those first three words – WE THE PEOPLE!

JUST A SECOND

It's only a minor thing – just a small, barely significant item of procedure in the sequence of events which occur during formal decision-making – the second. Despite its minor importance, it is not at all impossible that highly essential matters were not properly addressed because that one little item — just a single word — "Second!" was unheard. But was it necessary? A lot of confusion exists about the second and this essay is an attempt to clarify at least some of it.

What was the origin of this procedure? Why?

I wanted to know, but I looked in vain in Darwin Patnode's admirable *A History of Parliamentary Procedure*, I researched through several dictionaries, I consulted parliamentary authorities from Luther Cushing to Hugh Cannon, from Jefferson's *Manual* to Robert, Sturgis, Demeter, and Deschler. I sought information from McMonagle and Pfister and from Riddick and Butcher. In every case, I was informed about how the process of "seconding" was used, but nowhere was there any information about how it came to exist.

So, let's synthesize! When there is no available history, it seems appropriate to make some logical assumptions.

I believe that long ago, when a leader such as King Arthur wanted a job done, he would assemble his knights and ask for volunteers.

"Oh, good, Sir Percival," he might say, "thank you for offering to help. You are my first choice for the task. And, Sir Geoffrey, as my second choice," he could add, "I want you to accompany him as a backup in case something goes wrong."

Thus Percival and Geoffrey, King Arthur's first and second would ride off to slay a dragon or some such thing. According to my dictionary, the role of Geoffrey, the "second," is in accord with the definition "A supporter to a combatant in a duel or boxing match."

In another century, according to more than one account, an affront to a lady or an implication of cowardice might earn a gauntlet across the face or, in gentler times a slap with a glove, followed by a statement that,

"My second shall call upon you this eventide."

And a duel would follow. The seconds, the supporters, would make all arrangements for a meeting (probably at dawn at some isolated place) where the principals would eventually attempt to wound or kill each other in the name of honor. Their seconds would stand by to insure that all was fair and proper according to the rules of the day. A second would not necessarily agree that a duel was the appropriate action, but would be present to support his friend. Unless there was some terrible breach of etiquette, no second would actually take part in the duel. The second was present only for support — to be sure that the rules were followed.

True or not, this assumed "history" points to a tradition which has been brought into parliamentary practice in modern times. When someone wishes to place some action before an assembly, it is appropriate that someone else, a "second," provide support. As in dueling days, the second does not necessarily agree with the proposed course of action, but is supporting the proposer's right to present his idea according to the rules of the day.

Unfortunately, this concept has become distorted and the common belief appears to assert that someone who seconds a motion is in complete agreement with it. The contrary may be true. By seconding a proposal, a person is indicating that the proposed action may be of interest to the assembly and that details concerning it should be discussed. After discussion, however, the supporter may very well be opposed to the motion and may vote against it.

In his non-traditional *Book of Procedures*, Joel Welty avoids confusion. He never mentions motions or seconds and writes only of proposals and support.

When a member makes a proposal to the meeting, chances are that half the members are woolgathering or ogling some other member whose appearance strikes their fancy. The chair therefore repeats the proposal — if any member has called out "Support!" — and says "It has been proposed and supported that we spend $300 for fireworks..." If no one calls out support for the proposal, the president waits a brief moment — just a hesitation, really — before saying, "Anyone support this?

If not, he adds, "The proposal will not be considered because it has not been supported." Thus meetings are protected against spending time on proposals that appeal only to a single member.

Robert is even more explicit:

> A second merely implies that the seconder agrees that the motion should come before the meeting and not that he necessarily favors the motion. A member may second a motion (even if using the word "support" as indicated above) because he would like to see the assembly go on record as rejecting the proposal ...[5]

It is commonly believed that parliamentary tradition will not allow the proposer of a motion to speak about it until it has been seconded and stated by the Chair. It is not always understood that there is no absolute requirement for a second. The reason behind compelling one is that the assembly should not be subjected to motions that have the support of only one member.

Even if there is no second, once the motion has been stated by the Chair and debate has begun, the Chair has, in effect, ruled that there is apparent support for the motion and that a formal second is unnecessary.[6]

If the Chair is certain that a motion meets with wide approval but members are slow in seconding it, he can state the question without waiting for a second.[7]

Occasionally, a motion fails to obtain a second, yet in the opinion of the Chair, it is a relevant motion and worthy of consideration by the group. Under such circumstances the Chair may make a statement to this effect, "While there was no second to this motion, it is the Chair's opinion that we should examine this matter before dismissing it completely. Is there any objection? (Pause) Hearing none, the Chair recognizes the maker of the motion to open discussion."

Rather than describing procedure for use when there is no second, Ray Keesey specifically excludes the second:

Motions need not be seconded. The requirement of a second is largely a waste of time. What member is so destitute of friends that he can't find one willing to second his motion? The traditional justification for requiring a second is that at least two members should support a motion to justify its consideration. ... There is nothing essentially wrong with the practice of seconding. It is simply unnecessary.[8]

Riddick and Butcher have a different point of view and suggest a wholly new procedure. They object to the traditional procedure that requires that a motion that has been proposed, seconded, and stated by the Chair must be opened for discussion by the assembly. They propose the "Question of Consideration."

When a main motion is made, any member, without recognition, has a right to address the chair and say, "Mr. President, I rise to question the consideration of this motion." The fact that the Chair has stated the question or that discussion has begun does not prevent a member from raising a question of consideration. This right is retained until some action has been taken.

When a member raises a question of consideration, the chair must put it to a vote immediately by stating, "Is it the will of the assembly to consider this motion at this time?"[9]

The rationale for this motion is that three persons (one, the maker; two, the seconder; and three, the Chair who states it) have the right to impose their will on a majority of the assembled voters as has been traditional. Why should three members at a meeting of many be empowered to determine what the membership should take time to discuss?

-o0o-

All this sums up the role of the second in contemporary parliamentary usage.

Usually, when a motion is made, it is seconded and then stated by the Chair.

If no second is made, the Chair may dismiss the motion without any consideration, or, if the Chair believes the motion of value to the assembly, he may allow it to be opened for discussion without a second, pending objection.

When a motion is proposed, whether seconded or not, an "Objection to Consideration" may be raised, requiring a favorable majority vote of the assembly prior to consideration.

Is there anything else? Oh, hold on just a second (unit of time)! I almost forgot! A second is never required for a motion which is presented to an assembly as a recommendation of a committee.

And there's another second (unit of numerical sequence) usually forgotten rule: A second is never required for a motion made in a meeting of a committee or board, even when made by the Chair.

-o0o-

Just for fun, what is a second of angular measurement?[10]

ALL ABOUT THE GORDIAN KNOT

I have a legend for you.

Once upon a time, in a far distant land, there lived a great king. He had enormous wealth in gold and precious jewels, his kingdom extended from horizon to horizon, his ships traveled across the seas, his armies were more powerful than any others, and there was peace across all the land. He was Gordias, lord of Persia, and ruler of the whole world. Or so it was told.

Mighty in warfare and wise in government, but Gordias had no successors. During his long reign, his brothers had not survived the many struggles with wild tribes in the desert and his sons had been killed in battles with foreign invaders. And the great king felt that Death was close upon him. Or so it was told to me.

Gordias caused a royal chariot to be brought to him. As it was placed before him, he commanded that an ox-yoke be balanced across its tongue. Then, with a cord of silk and gold, Gordias tied the yoke to the tongue with an intricate knot. The ends of the cord were so tangled within that there appeared no manner in which the knot could be loosened.

Then Gordias spoke to his people, "Let no man touch this knot until the day of my death. When I am gone, let it be known across the land that he who separates the ox-yoke from the tongue of the chariot shall inherit my crown and shall rule in my place over my kingdom. He shall be the ruler of the world!" And so it was told.

When it was announced to the world that the king was dead, men came from lands far and near, from places known and unknown, from forest trees and from desert sands, each one in an effort to earn the kingdom of Gordias. And each one studied the interweaving of the cord of gold and silk and then would try and try again, and fail, for the knot was wondrous complex.

Time passed and the ox-yoke remained knotted to the chariot tongue, the land diminished, and the people were sorely pressed.

From a nation to the West, came a vast army, led by a young king, Alexander of Macedonia. To him no desert was too wide, no mountain was too high, no battle was too fierce, no challenge was too hard. When told of the Knot of Gordias, Alexander cried, "Take me to this puzzle forthwith!" And when he saw it, he studied it for an instant only, and then, with one slashing blow of his broadsword, he severed the silken cords of the knot and the ox-yoke fell to the ground.

"Behold!" cried his men, "Alexander is the ruler of the world!" And they called him "Great" and the people of the land bowed before him and shouted his name and the land flourished and all those who had gone before hailed him as their leader.

But Alexander the Great wept, for he was the ruler of the world — the whole world — and there could be nothing more for him to conquer. Or so it was told to me.

Since that time, this tale has been told and retold. And the Gordian Knot has become part of our language, for now, when affairs of any nature become so complex and tangled that no one knows the beginning from the end nor any way in which the problem can be solved, we can declare it a Gordian Knot.

There are many occasions when members at a meeting become so absorbed with the solving of a problem or the planning of an event that proposals are amended and modified, referred to committees, postponed, debated and delayed. Eventually, no one is quite sure where the pathway to the desired goal might be, nor what exactly is the next step to take, and the poor secretary has no idea about what might be happening.

When this happens to you, remember that Alexander the Great can come to the rescue. With one swift blow, the tangle can be resolved and the pathway cleared of all obstruction.

You can cut the Gordian Knot. How? You simply take a short route directly back to the original main motion that started the confusion. Someone might say, at a time when the situation became chaotic, "I move that we suspend the rules and return to discussion on the main motion." Or the presiding officer, who is as confused as anyone, might very well say, "Unless there is an objection, we will cut the Gordian Knot, forget all the confusion we have created, and take up the original main motion again."

You will find no mention of the Gordian Knot in most parliamentary codes, but careful examination of *Robert's Rules* shows that:

> When an assembly wishes to do something that
> it cannot do without violating one or more of its
> regular rules, it can adopt a motion to Suspend
> the Rules interfering with the the proposed ac-
> tion — provided the proposal is not in conflict
> with the organization's bylaws ... or the funda-
> mental principles of parliamentary law.[11]

The motion to *Suspend the Rules* is well known, but the concept of the Gordian Knot is unfamiliar to most parliamentarians. It was Dr. Floyd Riddick, Parliamentarian Emeritus of the United States Senate, who introduced it at a meeting of the Board of Directors of the American Institute of Parliamentarians in 1976. However, while *Riddick's Rules of Procedure*, like all the other authorities, discusses the motion *To Suspend the Rules*, it never mentions the Gordian Knot except a brief description on page 95 of an unorthodox and seldom-used procedure for expunging records "to avoid the exposure of situations which would be helpful to no one and embarrassing to everyone involved."

Only in the fourth revision of the Sturgis *Standard Code of Parliamentary Procedure* is there a specific description of the Gordian Knot as we know it today. In a paragraph entitled "The Gordian Knot" it states:

> Sometimes the parliamentary situation in a meeting becomes so confused that neither the chair nor the members can figure out how to proceed. In such cases, debate can become bitter and counterproductive, focusing on procedure rather than on substance.
>
> In such a case, a member might say, ".... I believe it would be best if we were to cancel out everything that has been done on this motion and start over again from the beginning, permitting the motion to be resubmitted in whatever form the maker wishes. I move that the rules be suspended to permit this."[12]

Such a motion usually will be passed by general consent because members on both sides of the question are likely to be equally frustrated and will welcome a way out

Only one other code mentions the parliamentary Gordian Knot. In my book, *The Majority Rules*, I included a brief description of the technique in the Glossary. Unlike *The Standard Code of Parliamentary Procedure*, which cancels even the main motion and allows the maker to start anew, my version eliminated all the intervening subsidiary motions but retains the original main motion. There are arguments in favor of both procedures.

However, either one will eliminate confusion. If the proposal has any significant value to the assembly, *The Standard Code* makes necessary a new proposal of the original main motion or a modified version of it, whereas my recommendation eliminates the chaos but returns directly to the main motion that is pending. If the assembly does not wish to become involved with it again, it can easily be withdrawn.

Whichever method is preferred, the Gordian Knot can solve the problem.

TO VOTE OR TO CONSENT?

In another essay, I stressed the social responsibility which requires every good citizen to participate in group decision-making by voting with both intelligence and knowledge. Having made that point, I now suggest that as a process, voting may be very bad.

There can be no question that under many circumstances, a decision on a controversial issue can be reached only by voting. When time is limited or when opposing opinions appear to be fixed, it may well be that only battleaxes or ballots can restore equanimity. In circumstances where vast numbers of participants are involved, such as a national election, we can reach a decision only by resorting to a vote with the hope that it will be made with factual knowledge and intelligence.

A vote does decide but it does not resolve the conflict. A requirement to vote compels an individual to assume a position — to take a stand either for or against a proposal. Human nature being what it is, we frequently form an opinion based on initial impressions and, once it is formed, refuse to contemplate any evidence in opposition. Before actually committing ourselves to a specific position, we should turn toward each side (and perhaps, even toward other alternatives), and listen to all the arguments in an effort to grasp enough facts to determine the best possible course of action. When we finally decide upon an appropriate solution, we should remain open-minded but instead, often stop investigating and resist those who would make us change.

Surely, if we could interrupt the process while every participant was still open-minded and receptive, it might mean that whatever decision we reached would be at least acceptable to the greatest number. In any group faced with a controversy, there will be extremists who have unalterable opinions, either pro or con, and many who are undecided. If required to vote, however, everyone will be forced into "yes" and "no" groups, even though many members might continue to see good points on both sides of the question. Unfortunately, many decisions are made in this fashion with the result that a few are elated, a few are frustrated, and the remainder accepts the decision with apathy, little commitment, and the attitude that "well, that's done. Maybe we did the right thing."

It might have been far more satisfactory had the decision been made without a vote. It might have been better if the decision could have been made by consensus — if the participants had agreed to accept the decision by "general consent." The group as a whole would feel committed to the decision because, as a whole, they had consented to it, possibly despite some misgivings. And they did not undergo a divisive vote!

But didn't they? Isn't deciding to agree a vote? Not really.

A vote is defined as "A formal expression of preference for a candidate for office or for a proposed resolution of an issue." (*The American Heritage Dictionary of the English Language*) Obviously the key word in the definition is "formal." By informally reaching for consensus, no individual is forced to "take a side." The group is not divided and contentious, but *informally* agreeing to a course of action. With a vote, antagonism becomes crystallized. When agreement is reached by common consent, some dissatisfaction may exist, but there will be no formal separation of the group into "majority" and "minority." Robert (page 53) says that the procedure is legitimate because "it is in accord with the principle that rules are designed for the protection of a minority and generally need not be strictly enforced when there is no minority to protect."

Parliamentary authorities are unanimous that obtaining agreement concerning an issue is a function of leadership. Doing so informally, by consensus, is a technique which has been used successfully for many years by Quakers and Indians, and is typical of the town meetings of New England.

The procedure is simple and may be applied to any motion, but for obvious reasons serves best and most easily when, in the opinion of the presiding officer, the issue before the assembly is of a non-controversial nature. When everyone is favorably disposed, business may be transacted expeditiously and time is saved. However, this cannot be assumed by the presiding officer but must be determined by member participation.

An example of such a case might exist when, amidst considerable repetitive, tiresome argument on a motion, a member moves to limit all further debate to ten minutes. After this is seconded, the leader may respond, "It has been moved and seconded to limit debate to ten minutes. *Is there any objection?*" If even one person does object, the question of limits must be put to a vote, but without objection, the presiding officer announces that by general consent, further debate on the pending question is limited to ten more minutes.

When no motion has been made, the presiding officer personally may propose action by general consent, even though this may appear to permit the leader to make a motion. The questions "Is there any objection?" or "Unless there is objection ...?" are magic keys which change dictatorship into leadership by allowing the assembly to participate in the decision. They also enable the presiding officer to change procedure, even under antagonistic conditions.

A motion has been made which is unpopular and does not receive a second. Nevertheless, the chair believes that the proposal deserves examination and discussion and should not be dismissed summarily. "The motion has been made that we increase our annual dues. Perhaps this should be explained. Unless there is objection, (pause to be certain none exists) I shall recognize the proposer." Even if only one person objects, a vote must be taken.

Genuine leadership can be demonstrated, confusion avoided and considerable time saved when the presiding officer says something like, "Since there is no further business, and unless there is an objection, (pause to be sure) this meeting is adjourned." (Viewing this analytically, the chair has moved and seconded the motion to adjourn, asked for and received the vote, and announced the result — all in one sentence and in less than fifteen seconds!)

In such an example, and by including the magic phrase ". . . unless there is an objection," the leader has used consensus to avoid that ridiculous and time-wasting question, "Do I hear a motion to adjourn?" (Dr. Gregg Phifer, CPP, a nationally known parliamentary writer, insists that this is really asking about the leader's ability to hear.)

Riddick and Butcher (page 194) describe two classes of general consent. The first has to do with the correct handling of a non-controversial main motion; the second with the techniques for establishing a procedure for the disposition of a number of items of business. Sturgis (page 136) prefers the term "general consent" rather than "unanimous consent" because the latter may be confused with "unanimous vote," which means that a vote was actually taken and everyone voted the same way. While "unanimous consent" implies that no one objects even though no formal vote was taken, "general consent" is, she feels, more precise.

Robert discusses "unanimous consent" in thirty-nine different sections by listing various specific procedures when consensus can be or must be applied. For example, on page 383, Robert requires consent in order to turn the leadership of the meeting over to anyone other than the vice-chairman, and on page 51, to introduce a motion without recognition by the presiding officer. He also points out that a requirement for a two-thirds vote can be satisfied in this manner (page 53).

Cannon (page 26) suggests using general consent to correct errors in a fashion similar to the technique known as "the Gordian Knot." He tells of the inadvertent oversight of a properly introduced proposed amendment to a pending motion at a convention. The next day the chair stated in effect, "We made a mistake here at the podium. This proposed amendment should have been recognized. If there is no objection, we will go back to the point in the debate on the main motion where I should have permitted the member to present his amendment." (This was done even though the main motion under question had been voted on and adopted the day before.)

This use of general consent eliminated the requirement for a motion for reconsideration, a second, debate, and a formal vote on the reconsideration. Demeter (page 175) suggests that general consent may be used for any motion, proceeding or request that the assembly cares to allow even though it is out of order when proposed, provided that action does not violate the bylaws.

General consent as an efficient time saver is well-known by experienced parliamentarians but is too frequently overlooked by presiding officers who rely only upon long-forgotten high school parliamentary instruction. Contemporary parliamentary authorities encourage its use as evidenced by the examples above: *Robert's Rules of Order, Newly Revised*, the Sturgis *Standard Code of Parliamentary Practice*, and *Riddick's Rules of Procedure*. In addition, there are many others including AIP's *Fundamentals of Parliamentary Law and Procedure* (page 273); Farwell's *Majority Rules* (page 21); Cannon's *Rules of Order* (pages 43-44 and 124-25); *Demeter's Manual of Parliamentary Law and Procedure* (pages 309-10); and Keesey's *Modern Parliamentary Practice* (page 133).

By pointing out the possible applications of the "General Consent" procedure, I hope that I have demonstrated yet another way in which the traditional and confusing insistence upon insignificant yet complex details can be eliminated from the conduct of business at meetings. No one goes to a meeting to listen to lectures about parliamentary procedure (except parliamentarians). They go there to conduct business efficiently. While the rules of procedure can move things fairly and effectively, just as the rules of football make the game fair and effective, no one goes to a football game just to see if the rules are obeyed. Possibly, were the rules of football as complicated as those of parliamentary procedure, the game might never be played!

Too often we complain that parliamentary procedure is frequently not used or misused at times when correct and appropriate use would have made a significant improvement in both the conduct and the outcome of business. The solution lies in simplification, a remedy advocated strongly by Robert English, founder of the American Institute of Parliamentarians, and endorsed by many of its members who continue to stress it today.

Parliamentary procedure should be an easy-to-understand, fair-to-all method of doing business in meetings. It should exist only to provide simple and understandable rules for that purpose. General consent is one of the procedures available to attain that goal.

TRUST AND PROCEDURE

My philosophy of parliamentary simplicity is founded upon the belief that when people trust each other, there can be a simple way to get the job done. This stems from my observation that in an atmosphere of real trust, even complex problems can be resolved without complicated procedures, but without trust, no parliamentary code will suffice.

A well-known but loosely knit organization held a convention at which members obviously did not know other members or the rules of order very well. Even though the general intent of the meeting was not complicated and was understood by all, it became obvious from questions and interruptions that the group did not really trust its leadership. The meeting adjourned, its work incomplete, when many members departed, understandably frustrated.

I strongly believe in the relationship between trust in leadership and parliamentary procedure. It is true that complex issues may require complex procedures; it is true that conflicting points of view cannot always be easily reconciled. But unless the members of a group trust their leaders and unless they trust the processes by which their leaders endeavor to guide them toward their objectives, they can achieve nothing.

There is little that can be done about developing trust among individuals. That rests upon a mysterious combination of personality, physical appearance, initial impression, reputation and other intangibles that I shall not attempt to analyze. There is, however, much that can be done to increase the trust that people have in parliamentary practice.

I believe that the problem can be attacked from three directions, by developing understanding through education, by increasing respect by describing the influence parliamentary procedure has had upon past and current events, and by building confidence through actual experience. As people gain greater understanding, respect for and confidence in parliamentary procedure, I think they will trust it as a tool for effective organizational accomplishment.

Perhaps the first step we might take in our educational drive might be to find a new, more attractive designation for our subject (see "NAME CHANGE?" on page 91). In my opinion, however, a greater problem lies in the traditional words and phrases so bewildering to the average club member. As long as our vocabulary is embroidered with motions to adjourn to an adjourned meeting or to go into a quasi-committee of the whole, we should expect resistance. As long as students must memorize charts and rules that govern motions of questionable practicality, we can expect apathy.

In my opinion, it is far more essential that people understand the logical reasoning behind a rule than the rule itself. It is far more important that a club member understands that a decision made by the leader may be questioned and even over-ruled than that the member uses the exact wording prescribed by some parliamentary authority.

Respect for parliamentary procedure will develop as people begin to appreciate that it is not just a tool for lawyers and legislators but for every group with objectives it hopes to reach. An analytic look at events, both current and historical, would reveal an enormous number of cases when appropriate parliamentary activity made a difference.

The First Amendment to our Constitution guarantees our right to assemble for any peaceable purpose. Regardless of what that purpose might be, there can be no hope of accomplishing it unless some degree of order is established. Without order, an assembly is a crowd, a chaotic unorganized mob that cannot survive or accomplish anything. Some system of rules must exist.

When everyone speaks at once, nobody can hear anything. A rule must be established and accepted that while everyone has the right to speak, only one person may speak at a time. Only then can the group stop marching simultaneously in all directions. Only when it is established and accepted that every member has equal rights and obligations can the group function as a unit rather than as a crowd of independent entities.

Even more important to the general public is the relationship of parliamentary procedure to group decision-making. We Americans are joiners, belonging to millions of organized units of every shape and structure imaginable. Almost daily, we are involved in making decisions in these groups, and to do so, we must use some form of parliamentary procedure.

Many times the procedures aren't done exactly as some parliamentary authority would have prescribed, but if they are done fairly and with due regard for the rights of others concerned, they will be recognized as a modified form of proper procedure.

Our respect for parliamentary procedure can only increase as we realize not only how much it has affected the way in which we interact with others, but also how closely it is affiliated with courtesy, tact, common sense and human dignity. It could be defined as an accepted code of tact and everyday courtesy applied when a number of people gather together to consider common problems and make group decisions which demand some form of action.

I have touched briefly upon understanding and respect, two of the three aspects of the program I advocate for building trust in parliamentary procedure. The third facet, confidence, is far easier to write about, but much more difficult to provide, for unfortunately, unlike understanding and respect, confidence cannot be taught. It can be learned only through observation and experience.

Even more unfortunate, far too many people have had experience of a less than satisfactory nature. Frequently, it is a mixture of semi-forgotten lessons from high school and what someone guessed was the right thing to do. Uncertain wandering in the wilderness of parliamentary procedure might adequately serve the presiding officer of some organization where social informality was the only objective, but it cannot inspire trust in the process. Far too many half-remembered (but better forgotten) procedures are encountered in such distorted form that they have become meaningless, and many ill-informed but self-styled "parliamentarians" speak out primarily to inflate their own self-images rather than to inform the public.

Effective parliamentary procedure is possible only in an atmosphere of trust – trust between the members and the leader, trust between the members and the procedures employed by the leader to enable the group to reach its goals, and trust in the procedures themselves.

Trust in the appropriate application of parliamentary law by trusted leaders is a fundamental element of national democracy.

WHO SAYS IT TAKES TWO-THIRDS?

Every presiding officer has been required to maneuver the members of his organization to the brink of a decision, only to be faced with the question, "Is this motion decided by an ordinary majority or does it require a two-thirds majority vote?" With experience, the chair learns that while an ordinary majority can decide any main motion and most procedural motions, there are a few which, according to some authorities, need a "super majority vote" of two-thirds or, in special cases, even larger, such as three-fourths or even nine-tenths.

Usually, when the parliamentary authority has prescribed a two-thirds majority vote, the experienced presiding officer announces the requirement and asks voters to stand or otherwise indicate their vote in a manner which can be counted if necessary (although a counted vote is not otherwise required). When the chairman has made that announcement, the members rarely question the requirement. Both the leader and the members passively accept the dictum — a two-thirds majority vote is required for approval. No one ever raises his hand to ask, "WHO SAID SO AND WHY?"

Maybe I am a maverick — maybe I'm just unable to accept rules that do not appear to be logical. There are far too many rules in existence now for which we can find no logical reason. Yet, parliamentarians teach that for each of the fundamental principles of good parliamentary procedure, a sound reason exists. That makes sense to me.

For example, we teach that only one subject can be discussed at a time. Now, that is a rule that makes sense. Who could possibly follow a conversation that simultaneously revolved around a fund-raising dance, a bus trip for members to the state legislature, and a vote of confidence in the new treasurer?

In any examination of procedure, I am always curious about the reason why it exists. In many cases, parliamentary procedure follows a rule found in some edition of Robert's *Pocket Manual of Rules of Order for Deliberative Assemblies*. In many cases, I find myself asking, "Why did Robert include this rule in his book, and where did he get the idea?"

Too frequently, my search for answers to "Who and Why" leads only to frustration. Upon the publication of *Deschler's Rules of Order*, I corresponded with the author, Lewis Deschler, former Parliamentarian of the U. S. House of Representatives. I wanted to know why, in Section 44, did he state, "When a motion has been made and carried or lost, it shall be in order for any member of the majority on the same or succeeding day, to move for the reconsideration thereof..." In his reply, Mr. Deschler wrote, "Only a member of the majority can move for consideration *because that is the rule*." (emphasis HF). I questioned him because I wanted to know "Why.".. I don't think he answered my question.

Years ago, when I was just beginning to study parliamentary procedure, I was struck by a statement in *Learning Parliamentary Procedure* by Alice Sturgis. In a brief discussion of the future of organizations, Sturgis wrote:

> Groups tend, increasingly, to place more trust in the decisions of the majority. This belief in the wisdom of majority rule is the keystone of de-mocracy and of democratic procedure. Legisla-tive bodies have never required more than a majority vote for any procedural motion. There is a long line of court decisions which hold that

there are no rules of parliamentary law which require more than a majority vote on any motion.

This principle is likely to be followed in the not too far distant future by voluntary organizations. In fact, there are already some organizations that require no more than a majority for procedural votes, such as the motions to vote immediately and to suspend rules, which, since the Victorian period, have required a two-thirds vote.

She continued,

Organizations are becoming generally aware that every vote which is higher than a majority takes power *away* from the majority and gives it to a minority — and organizations resent being ruled by a minority.[13]

The new Sturgis, the *Standard Code of Parliamentary Procedure*, echoes this concept:

As a general rule, fewer than a majority should not be authorized to decide anything, and more than a majority should not be required for most decisions.[14]

Inspired by Sturgis and by the parliamentary principle that the rights of every member of an organization are equal in every way to the rights of every other member, I have written much and spoken frequently and at length about the contradiction that can be seen in every parliamentary authority. All of them *endorse* the principle of majority rule. The United States House of Representatives is guided by Jefferson's *Manual*, in which we find the frequently quoted:

The voice of the majority decides; for the *lex majoris partis* is the law of all councils, elections, &c. where not otherwise expressly provided.

George Hills, in *Managing Corporate Meetings*, tells us that:

Our government and our institutions rest on the principle that controlling power is vested in the majority. In the absence of any provision by law to the contrary, the will of any community or association, body politic or corporate, is properly declared only by the voice of the majority.[15]

Robert faces the issue squarely, despite his insistence upon certain super-majority requirements.

The basic principle of decision in a deliberative assembly is that, to become the act or choice of the body, a proposition must be adopted by a *majority vote*; that is, direct approval — implying assumption of responsibility for the act — must be registered by more than half of the members present and voting on the particular matter.[16]

In his *Manual of Legislative Procedure*, Paul Mason states,

1. A fundamental and seemingly universal principle is that at least a majority of the vote cast is required to make decisions for a group.

2. If powers were given to a minority, the question would immediately rise as to what minority? In any group there can be but one majority, but there may be many different minorities.

3. To require more than a majority to reach any decision confers on less than a majority the power to block or prevent a decision.[17]

Despite these statements, many parliamentary authorities have continued to insist that some motions require that a minimum of two-thirds of those who vote must be in favor for the motion to be approved. The new fourth edition of the Sturgis *Standard Code* lists only three such motions, plus one other which requires a two-thirds vote under some conditions. The new Robert, on the other hand, lists twelve motions which always require two-thirds and ten others which do under some conditions and not under others.

All right, let's get to the "Why and Who."

In his *Rules of Order*, Deschler states that the requirement for a vote that is larger than a majority is "intended to ensure widespread support on fundamental issues," which I believe is a logical and understandable reason. However, he continues by pointing out that this also "makes it possible for the minority to thwart the will of the majority."[18]

Robert tells us, in a list of basic fundamentals, that parliamentary law is based on five principles, among which is a "regard for the rights of the minority, especially a strong minority — greater than one-third." There is nothing magic about that fractional portion. Why should we be more concerned about a minority of one-third than about a minority of just one person? Surely due regard for the rights of every individual should be considered by any group concerned with intelligent decision-making.

> As a compromise between the rights of the individual and the rights of the assembly, the principle has been established that a two-thirds vote is required to adopt any motion that: (a) suspends or modifies a rule of order previously adopted; (b) prevents the introduction of a question for consideration; (c) closes, limits or extends the limits of debate; (d) closes nominations or the polls, or otherwise limits the freedom of nominating or voting; or (e) takes away membership or office.[19]

45

This thinking is obviously accepted by Cannon, by Deschler, by Demeter, by Hills, by Mason, by Keesey, and even by Sturgis, and, to my dismay, Riddick and Butcher! WHO SAYS TWO/ THIRDS? Evidently, almost everyone except Farwell! And even I fall in line to a degree. In my book and in my teaching, I have emphasized that any group is free to adopt any rule which best suits their particular organization and if they feel that certain motions should require a super-majority, they are free to adopt such a requirement as a standing rule. This makes sense to me.

But even that doesn't really answer the question "Who?" I just quoted Robert who said, "The principle has been established..." That falls short of telling *who*. My dictionary says that "to establish" means, among other things, "to cause to be recognized and accepted without question." Well, I, personally, do not "accept without question." Any time the majority of a group decides to do something, a smaller number should not have the right to prevent that action unless the larger group agrees to this with full understanding of the unfortunate possibilities.

Every day, we may read in our newspapers how small, even minute, aggressive and articulate minorities have caused delays and even cancellation of programs initiated and approved by majorities. In western Colorado, a massive water storage project which would bring desperately needed water to the desert lands on which we have very generously relocated the Apache, Hopi and Navajo Indians was stalled for years. A very small group of environmentalists tried to convince us that the continued existence of the squawfish was more important to the world than were a few thirsty native Americans. The project had been approved and funded by the national government in conjunction with the states of Colorado, New Mexico and Arizona. Wildlife specialists had declared the squawfish itself a "trash fish". Far more than a two-thirds majority had spoken in favor of the project, yet a small minority almost caused its cancellation.

A basic credo of parliamentary law emphasizes that while the majority rules, nevertheless, the minority must be heard. Obviously, in the pre-decision period, every member, regardless of his position concerning the desirability of the proposal, has the right to speak and be heard. However, when the decision is reached by the vote of the majority of the members present who are legally entitled to vote, the decision must be accepted by all members. *Acceptance does not mean that all opposition should cease.*It does not imply that valid reasons for dispute should be brushed aside and forgotten. Acceptance does mean that the organization will move in a specific direction until, by majority vote, the group decides on some other course of action. When one party becomes the majority in our national legislature, the other party becomes the "loyal opposition." Our Senators and Congressmen are all American citizens, and what they do is, at least from their point of view, in the best interests of our nation. And that makes sense to me.

And one of the things our Senators do, in furthering their programs "in the best interests of the nation," is to invoke "cloture," a procedure which in non-Congressional language is the motion to "Vote Immediately" or to "Call for the Previous Question." According to Dr. Floyd Riddick's book, *Senate Procedure*, cloture is a complex action which is initiated by sixteen Senators who sign a motion to "close the debate" and present it to the presiding officer. Following such notification, nothing happens regarding it until one hour after the Senate convenes on the following calendar day. At that time, the presiding officer shall:

> ... lay the motion before the Senate and direct that the Clerk call the roll, and upon ascertainment that a quorum is present, the Presiding Officer shall, without debate, submit to the Senate by a yea-and-nay vote the question: "Is it the sense of the Senate that the debate shall be brought to a close?"[20]

A three-fifths affirmative vote "of the Senators duly chosen and sworn — except on a measure to amend the Senate rules, in which case the necessary affirmative vote shall be two-thirds of the Senators present and voting —" is required to invoke cloture.

Thus, if sixteen Senators, out of a total group of one hundred, desire to stop the debate, even though it is possible that eighty-four want to keep talking about it, the motion, after a procedural delay, will go to the floor for a decision. At that time, if all one hundred Senators, "duly chosen and sworn" are present and voting, forty-one Senators can defeat the motion. If it is a "measure to amend the rules of the Senate," thirty-four Senators can defeat it.

What is so significant about "two-thirds"? In a group of six, four is both a majority and a two-thirds majority. In a group of one hundred, a two-thirds majority means that at least sixty-seven members must vote in favor of a proposition while thirty-three may vote against it. Suppose that thirty-four vote against it and sixty-six vote for it. In that case, the motion does not carry and the votes of the members of the minority have been given a value almost twice as great as the votes of the majority.

In a society of equals, no person's vote should be worth more than any other's. In a society of equals, the rights of a member are equal to and neither superior nor inferior to the rights of any other member. To me, that is what democracy means. I feel that any controversy should be discussed and debated in a meeting, and, if necessary, compromised in order to bring about the most favorable solution possible for all members.

If one member or group of members should attempt to control a meeting by threats, coercion or violence, the sky would fall and every knowledgeable member would be on his feet in an effort to control the chaos. But if that same small group could control the actions of the group by resorting to a rule that provides that only the vote of a two-thirds majority will prevail, many of us would sit back down saying, "Oh, yes, that's the rule." Well, it may be the rule, but it doesn't make sense to me.

What I am talking about is not some obscure philosophical compromise, as Robert said, "between the rights of the assembly and the rights of the individual." What I am really talking about is the fact that under certain circumstances, it appears that the minority has more rights than the majority. What I am really talking about is not MAJORITY RULE, but the TYRANNY OF THE MINORITY!

As we look around our present-day society, the phenomenon of minority supremacy seems ever more dominant. Our courts seem far more concerned with the rights of the criminal than of the victim; the right of millions of Boy Scouts to trust in God is challenged by a few who have no god; militant feminists have disrupted football locker rooms and military institutions; sincere medical researchers have been interrupted by an equally sincere few who believe that no animal, even a rat, should be sacrificed to research in order to save a human life.

Not long ago, a handshake in Washington seemed to indicate that peace in the Middle East might become an actuality — that the Palestinians and the Israelis might live together in harmony. While the whole world watches and the leaders of both groups hope for mutual agreement, small minorities use the tactics of terror to delay if not defeat the hopes and desire of both majorities. In our own country, the violent tactics of small but sincere groups of anti-abortion activists have caused the murder of one doctor and the fear of death among others. I have been reminded that all too frequently, while we do respect the rights of minorities, some groups who are dedicated to some particular policy or issue believe that we are ignorant of that policy or minimize its importance. They argue that only by dramatic and sometimes violent actions can our "neglect" be brought into focus. Surely Dr. Kevorkian, a one-man minority, has brought the issue of euthanasia to our attention! The old saying that a "squeaking wheel gets the most oil" is very valid. But a single squeaky wheel should not derail the entire train! Intelligent discussion of the issue should take place without undue disturbance. The position and the rights of the majority as well as the minority should be understood. And, as a result, if the issue is significant, both sides should make appropriate adjustments — not because of fear, but because of respect for majority rule.

I have argued that there is no such thing as a majority — that our entire society is composed of a myriad of tiny, individual minorities, each with its own goals, its own rules and its own limitations. From time to time, groups of these minorities link together, sometimes in such number that they form a majority, to achieve a common objective, but that is just a fleeting, temporary thing which exists only long enough to reach the goal and then dissolves into its tiny component parts.

I see in this growth of minority power a final catastrophe when groups of minorities, each claiming to represent just a little bit more than one-third of the world, will establish the new order. No longer shall majority rule prevail — no longer will the people speak with a single voice but with a discordant babble! And the world will be governed by the one-third majority vote! There will be many who scoff at this statement, who feel that once again, Farwell is blowing smoke. There will be many who will agree that we have concentrated so much on the significance of the rights of the minority that the rights of the majority have become relatively insignificant, but most will argue that never, at least never in these United States, will we ever allow ourselves to be controlled by the power of the minority!

NO? Let's look back only a few years. In the 1968 presidential election, nearly seventy-three million voters cast ballots. If we consider the popular vote, disregarding the Electoral College, a candidate would have had to receive about 37 million votes to be elected. As it was, no candidate had more than 32 million. Richard Nixon was elected by a minority and it was a smaller minority of 10 million votes for George Wallace that controlled the election. In 1992, Bill Clinton received 43 million, seven hundred thousand votes. George Bush had 38 million. If either candidate had been able to claim the nearly twenty million votes for Ross Perot, we would have had a president with a "mandate from the majority." As it was, however, of the more than one hundred million citizens who voted, almost sixty million voted for a candidate other than Bill Clinton.

It doesn't make sense to me, but it is becoming more and more obvious. **Never underestimate the power of the minority!**

In this discussion, I have been concerned with the "Who and Why" of the two-thirds majority vote. I have identified those who endorse and foster this practice, but I do not feel that I have developed a satisfactory answer to either question. Certainly the roots of the two-thirds vote lies in antiquity, and the person or group who first established the concept will probably never be known. I have emphasized that Henry Robert, the parliamentary authority most responsible for enforcing the two-thirds vote within voluntary organizations, considered it a compromise. I can only repeat what others have said before me — that when the vote of a small group of members can delay or defeat the will of the majority of members, then equality of membership is non-existent. A compromise between the rights of the group and the rights of the individual may be the best possible answer, but it doesn't make sense to me, but it is becoming more and more obvious. **Never underestimate the power of the minority!**

GEORGE'S GOLF LESSON

There wasn't much excitement when the President recognized the chairman of the nominating committee.

As a matter of fact, there wasn't any excitement at all. The meeting was really dull. But nobody expected it to be exciting. Every one of the members present knew exactly what was going to happen.

It was time for the scheduled annual election of officers. And in the time-honored tradition of the organization, the only possible question revolved around the identity of the new man on the team. Three officers, each serving for one year, were always elected to the next highest position the following term. Thus trained personnel were always available and the continuity of the society would be preserved. Upon the expiration of the term of the President, the First Vice-President would be elected to fill that position, The Second Vice-President would step up to First, and the Third Vice-President would become the Second. Unlike the positions of Secretary, Treasurer, and Administrative Officer, who could be re-elected indefinitely to two-year terms, no President or Vice-President could succeed himself.

It was a very logical system and had been in effect for years. Usually, the outgoing President would select from a group of qualified juniors the individual who would fill the position of Third Vice-President in the new administration. There was a likely rumor going around that this year's candidate would be Henry, an obvious winner. In just four years, after gaining the necessary experience, he undoubtedly would assume the top responsibility of President.

This was fine with George. Everything was cut-and-dried and the meeting would be all finished before three-thirty, when he had a date to tee-off with Eric at the Country Golf Estates. He knew that as soon as the nominating committee completes its report, the President will thank them and then say, "You have heard the nominations. Wilbur Smith has been nominated for President for next year. Are there any other nominations for the office of President?" (George knew that there will not be any – it was hard enough to get Wilbur to agree to step up. It had been a long four years for him!} The President speaks again, "Are there any other nominations?" and repeats, "Are there any other nominations?"

It happened just like that. George knew it would.

To no one's surprise, there were no other nominations. Then, exactly as he had done for the last six years, one of the older members asked for recognition. "Mr. Chairman," he said, "I move that the nominations be closed, the rules be suspended, and the secretary be directed to vote a white ballot for Wilbur Smith for President." Three other members leaped to their feet to shout, "I second the motion." It took some time for the secretary to determine which member was to be recorded as the seconder.

George thought it wasn't necessary to record the name of the seconder.

The President said, "Very well, since there is no other nomination, a ballot vote is not required and we may vote by show of hands." He then asked for positive and then negative indications.

"Thank goodness," thought George, who was noticing that while things were moving, they were moving very slowly. He really wanted to get out on the golf course on this beautiful day.

The President announced that Wilbur Smith, having been duly elected, was the incoming President of the organization. He then stated, "You have heard the report of the nominating committee. Robert Muckle has been nominated for the office of First Vice-

President. Are there any other nominations? Are there any other nominations?" Several members smiled audibly at the unnecessary repetition. "Are there any other nominations?"

Again the member arose to move "that the nominations be closed, the rules suspended and the secretary directed to cast a white ballot." And the First Vice-President was declared elected. Things were moving right along, but George kept checking his watch. This meeting was important, but George wanted it to adjourn so that he could join his friends at the golf course.

By the time the nomination and election of the Second Vice-President was completed, even the presiding officer was grinning as he asked, again and again for other nominations.

Then came the moment of really high drama! The President asked the First Vice-President to take his gavel while he asked for recognition to make a nomination. The suspense was breathtaking – he nominated Henry! The Vice- President then asked for other nominations and after the traditional repetitions, the usual motion was made to close nominations, suspend the rules and instruct the secretary. After the motion had been officially seconded, he returned the gavel to the President. Without further delay, Henry was declared the victor!

Because that was the scheduled ending, George barely listened while the President announced the program for the following meeting, which, traditionally, included the installation of the new officers.

Everything went well and according to the custom established by years of nearly identical assemblies. But it was three-thirty and George was going to be late.

As he drove to the country club, George asked himself about all the ritualistic trappings that had made a totally predictable event so lengthy and boring. He felt that everyone in the room thought the ridiculous repetition and jumbled motions could have been omitted. He reminded himself that parliamentary procedure was supposed to expedite business, not to provide comedy.

First of all, was it necessary (or traditional?) to ask for other nominations *three* times? And how about that single three-part motion to close nominations, suspend the rules and then give instructions?

He was sure that things could be improved. He thought about it as he drove to the golf course, where he was luckily able to join his friends on the first hole.

-o0o-

According to most modern parliamentary authorities, there were many irregularities in the meeting, and George was sure there were several valuable lessons to be learned from his experience this afternoon.

Individually, those procedures that annoyed George were not greatly significant, but as a group, particularly when George was impatiently waiting for adjournment, they bothered him considerably.

First of all, George felt the triple repetition of the invitation for floor nominations was unnecessary. The entire membership, including the presiding officer himself, knew that there were no other nominations nor would there be any. In a large and noisy assembly, especially in the absence of an adequate public address system, George conceded, the continued repetitions might be valuable but in a small organization it was only a time-wasting practice and should be discontinued.

Under most circumstances, when a single motion is proposed which consists of several unrelated actions, it is customary to divide the motion into separate parts:

The motion to close nominations. Most authorities agree that this motion is not needed when the nomination is uncontested except as a signal that it was time to vote. Knowing, as he did that there would be no additions, the presiding officer could declare the nominations closed. When used to prevent nominations of undesirable but fully qualified members, it should not be permitted. Why lock a door if nobody wants to open it? This motion, too, George felt should be discontinued.

The motion to suspend the rules. It is customary to describe the specific rule that might be suspended at the time this motion is made, especially when many rules, such as the fundamentals of parliamentary law or bylaw provisions, cannot properly be suspended. In this case, it is possible that the bylaws might require a written, secret vote, and a suspension would be improper.

The motion to cast a white ballot. Many organizations vote, particularly on membership applications, by casting either a white "yes" ball, or a black ball. Obviously, when an applicant is "blackballed," membership is refused if a unanimous vote is required. However, George realized, when only one ballot is cast, with no opportunity for another, possibly different vote, it would mean that the total assembly voted unanimously for Henry. George knew that some members disliked Henry and probably would have voted against him. The single white ballot indicates that their negative votes were unimportant. While he might have been elected by a majority vote, Henry probably would not have been a unanimous choice.

There was also a delay while the name of the seconder was determined. While current practice still expects a motion to be seconded , every authority insists that the recording of the name of the seconder is unnecessary.

As he approached the first tee, George realized that his annoyance was directed at procedures that were improper according to parliamentary law. But he forgot (if he ever knew) the foundation of "parliamentary law." You see, there really isn't any such thing as "parliamentary law." There is no specific, clear definition of the term. It is a vague, formless body of rules that are founded on ancient usage and custom. With mutual agreement among all members, any organization can develop its own rules which, if applied equally and fairly to every member, are as legal as any other rules. When no specific regulation or bylaw exists, accepted custom and usage controls the approval of membership applications, the conduct of meetings, elections, etc.

Parliamentary law and what is considered "correct" procedure, is comprised of the voluntary self-imposed rules and customs that govern deliberative assemblies.

In other words, there is no law that prohibits the traditional procedures that George feels are incorrect and time wasting. No regulation requires them, either, but custom and tradition have established them and the members universally accept them

George felt that an event that should have been, despite the small size of the organization, an important and possibly inspiring ceremony, had been converted to a time-wasting, rather laughable event. He believed that it was tolerated, not because it formed a basis for a good administration, but because of traditions. Tradition and ancient ritual were important, and perhaps rightfully belonged in societies such as this, founded many years in the past by the leaders of the community. They initiated procedures and customs that were both logical and appropriate for the time, but with the passage of years, had become insignificant and, he felt, rather tiresome.

George learned quite a bit in his study of the election ceremony. First of all, it was clear that in an organization, with the approval of the membership, traditional behavior may provide a kind of framework upon which to erect procedures that might be unique to that group. Secondly, he learned that procedures that were clearly different from those prescribed by accepted modern parliamentary authorities are not necessarily wrong.

At the clubhouse, as George and his friends tallied their cards, he realized that he had also learned another lesson. A good golf score requires concentration on the game

THE PARLIAMENTARY PILLARS

Many years ago, T. E. Lawrence, known as Lawrence of Arabia, wrote a book entitled *Seven Pillars of Wisdom*. I do not remember much that I read in that book, but the title came into my mind and stayed there. Somehow the concept of columns of wisdom seemed important. Then I understood that I was relating the seven columns to the fundamentals of parliamentary law. As I conceive them, there are seven — and each of them is both wise and essential to anyone who might endeavor to function as a parliamentarian.

What are the seven pillars of parliamentary wisdom? My limited training in art suggests that to understand a "pillar," you start by examining those elements that give a full, three-dimensional completeness to the picture. From my point of view, those elements are the basic parliamentary principles and my concern here is to demonstrate how they function together to provide depth and greater understanding. In a painting. the artist endeavors to show that each detail exists as a part of the whole — that no one feature could exist alone.

Because my train of thought seemed involved with the title of Lawrence's book, I did a bit of research to determine its source and found it in the Bible, in Chapter Nine of the Book of Proverbs. It seems appropriate to quote a bit of it here.

> Wisdom has built her house; she has hewn out
> its seven pillars. She has set her table. She has
> sent out her maids and she calls from the highest
> point of the city,

> Come, eat my food and walk in the way of un-
> derstanding. ... Instruct a wise man and he will
> be wiser still; teach a righteous man and he will
> add to his understanding.

We are all residents of that house with the seven pillars, for as decision-makers, we deal with the principles of Ethics, Order, Equality, Justice, Majority Rule, Rights of the Majority and Rights of the Minority. It is of no concern that you favor Robert's *Rules* over Sturgis, that you use Keesey instead of Farwell as your parliamentary authority, or that Demeter's *Blue Book* answers all your questions — those seven pillars provide the strength, the foundation for what we teach, what we write and what we advise.

While we all recognize these pillars, these concepts, as important, I feel that we would do well to look more closely at each of them. After all, the proverb told us, "Teach a wise man and he will be wiser still; teach a righteous man and he will add to his understanding."

Since we are all both wise and righteous, we have everything to gain.

ETHICS

Let's start out with **Ethics**. There is a lot of talk about the ethical parliamentarian. Like many organizations, parliamentary associations such as the American Institute of Parliamentarians and the National Association of Parliamentarians have Codes of Ethics. The first parliamentary article I wrote, way back in 1972, was a short essay on "The Ethical Parliamentarian." But what do we really know about ethics?

Dictionaries define "Ethics" in many ways, but almost universally, they say that ethics is the study of the general nature of morals and of the specific moral choices to be made by the individual in his relationship with others. Ethics means the rules or standards governing conduct. The Code of Ethics of the American Institute of Parliamentarians is divided into four sections: professional employment; relationship with the public; conduct as a teacher of parliamentary procedure; and conduct as a member of the organization. I believe that the Preamble to the AIP Code is a positive statement that is worth far more attention than it has received:

> The American Institute of Parliamentarians believes in the worth and dignity of man. To this end, we recognize the supreme importance of respect, devotion to equal justice under law, the pursuit of truth and the nurture of democratic principles. AIP regards as essential to these goals the protection of freedom of speech and the guarantee of equal opportunity in all types of organizations for education in the use of parliamentary law. We accept our responsibility to practice our profession according to the highest ethical standards.

In essence, this means that parliamentarians must be impartial in judgment, knowledgeable about procedure, tolerant of opposition, enlightening to ignorance and courteous in their interpersonal relations. Maybe Ethics can be summed up as courteous, responsible impartiality.

ORDER

My dictionary defines "**Order**" in many ways such as "A condition of logical or comprehensible arrangement among the separate elements of a group" or "A condition of methodical or prescribed arrangement among component parts, such that proper functioning or appearance is achieved." The definition which I feel best suits our examination of the parliamentary perspective is, "Logical and customary procedure." Now we all know that there is a logical manner in which we do things. When we climb a flight of stairs we put foot first on the bottom step. The famous Chinese proverb says "The longest journey starts with a single step." Whoever heard of starting at the end of the twenty-second mile? There are some who read the last chapter of a mystery story first, and one lady I know enjoys her dessert so much that she always eats it first to be sure she has room for it. Like anything else, we can always find exceptions, but disorder, chaos and confusion almost invariably lead to inefficiency, misunderstanding and conflict, and loss of control.

Edmund Burke, in a 1791 letter to a British politician, wrote, "Good order is the foundation of all things." As we think of order, we think of the procedures we use to make decisions. John Dewey defined the orderly procedure of problem-solving in his 1910 book, *How We Think*, as a five-step procedure, which was an arrangement so that each step logically led to the final outcome.

Dewey's orderly progression of "reflective thinking" moved from the definition of the problem, the gathering of information, the development of plans and, finally, the acceptance or rejection of the best possible solution. And that final stage, the acceptance or rejection of solutions, is the arrival at a decision — a process that relies strongly on parliamentary procedure as an orderly method for success.

Too frequently, organizations, meeting in a large, general group, tackle all five of Dewey's procedures simultaneously with the result that an enormous amount of time is spent in defining the problem, gathering information and developing solutions — work properly accomplished successfully by committees, but deadly when attempted by a large group. And, far too frequently, the wasted time and individual frustration is blamed solely on parliamentary procedure, a tool designed only for the final stage, decision making.

In summary, parliamentary order means to do things in a logical manner and use tools for the purpose for which they were designed.

EQUALITY

Let's move on to **Equality**. It is quite true, unfortunately, that in our world today, enlightened though it may be, real equality does not exist except within limited areas and under limited circumstances. The Declaration of Independence states without equivocation that "... all men are created equal," and Section 9 of the first Article of the Constitution of the United States is adamant: "No Title of Nobility shall be granted by the United States." According to our law, we Americans live in a classless society where every child born is the equal of any other — which may be true, but it doesn't stay true. Somehow, we get categorized into different groups such as Christians or college graduates or Arabs or union members or Russians or lawyers or females or senior citizens or Republicans. It seems that while everyone in your own group may be equal, you rank the group as a whole higher than any other because **you** are in it. And if that isn't confusing enough, everyone belongs to several different groups. It is highly improbable that a Harvard Law School graduate would feel that a professional wrestler was his equal. — But if he were also a graduate of Harvard Law School, he might be quite acceptable. And it might be even better (or worse!) if he were a Democrat!

The parliamentary side of the coin can be stated fairly easily. Within any organization there will be as many *different* people as there are members. No two will be alike. They may belong to totally different categories, but within that specific organization they **must** be considered equal with equal rights, privileges and responsibilities. One member may belong to the country club, another might be on welfare, but as far as their mutual membership in the organization is concerned, there can be no difference between them. They are equal. As citizens of the United States of America, we are all equal in regard to our rights and responsibilities.

JUSTICE

The concept of **Justice** is closely related to equality. When a parliamentarian refers to justice, he is reminded again of our Constitution, which guarantees "justice for all" and provides protection against being deprived of life, liberty, or property without due process of law. No parliamentary rule can be considered legal or acceptable unless it applies equally to every member of the organization.

MAJORITY RULE

We need to concentrate now on the concept of **majority rule**. In *The Standard Code*, Alice Sturgis quotes from a letter written to Baron von Humboldt in 1817 by Thomas Jefferson:

> The first principle of republicanism is that the *lex majoris partis* is the fundamental law of every society of individuals of equal rights; to consider the will of the society enounced by the majority of a single vote, as sacred as if unanimous, is the first of all lessons in importance, yet the last which is thoroughly learnt.[21]

The philosophy behind majority rule is simple —— the will of the majority shall prevail. That can become reality, of course, only when the source of power lies within the society. Either a society is ruled by external power or by power originating within itself. External power is exemplified by authoritarian rule, frequently fortified with coercion, threats and violence. External power is usually held by a small group, or by a single individual, as in a dictatorship or the absolute monarchies of ancient days. Internal power, the power that comes from within the group and only with its consent, exists in an atmosphere of cooperation and trust.

When a society - whether it be a nation or a sewing circle - is governed by some external power, its members must act involuntarily and at the whim of the external power. They have no ability to decide upon the merits of their actions, and are required to follow orders or suffer some kind of penalty. Individual human rights are rarely considered — if they exist at all.

Internal power arises not from coercion and threat, but from consensus. Internal power is created with the consent of the members of the society, and is based upon the personal rights of each member, some small portion of which is voluntarily yielded for the mutual benefit of all members. Prehistoric man, alone, could not defeat the awesome sabre-tooth tiger, but banded together with others of his clan, he could be protected from the dangers of his world. But a portion of his personal independence had to be sacrificed to gain personal security.

The conflict between independence and unity is always with us. Just as ancient man had to join his brothers for security, we gain strength by joining our neighbors, both as individuals and as larger entities. Benjamin Franklin is credited with the remarks "If we don't hang together, we shall surely hang apart," and "United we stand, divided we fall!" Today, we have labor unions, political action committees, and a myriad of other organizations, for groups of people can accomplish easily and quickly what one person could not do in a lifetime.

Today, there is no better illustration of the conflict between independence and group strength than what has happened to the former Soviet Union. Once a great and fearsome giant, so strong that it was considered a threat to the peace and stability of the entire western world, it is now a collection of shadows of its former self, some fourteen or more individual countries, each struggling to establish its independence, each striving for the internal power necessary to attain democratic government of and by its people. It is unfortunate that fifty years of external power and control cannot be wiped away instantly — the changes to come in that vast area will be measured in years and decades rather than weeks.

In this country, thank God, we do have a fair degree of national and personal independence and security through group strength — at least for the time being. But we have less privacy — we have fewer opportunities to be alone with just ourselves or just our families. We have been forced to conform to various behavioral norms. If we like to swim, we can only do so in certain limited areas — if we want to stay in bed all day, we must first call the office to inform the others. We have sacrificed our personal right to independence in order to be part of a unified group from which we can gain strength enough to survive. And to be part of that group is to accept the behavioral norms of that group.

Accepting a group's norms means accepting the customs, rules and beliefs of most of the people within it. These customs and rules are developed from within the group, based on what **most** people believe is "right." Most people believe that public nudity is not acceptable, so we have an unwritten rule, and in many places a law, prohibiting it. Most people feel that obscene profanity is not acceptable, so we have rules about that. We, as individuals, may have the right to behave in certain ways, but in doing so, we may well be in conflict with the norms of the group. To be part of the group, we must conform to the rules and customs of most members of that group because what most of them believe is right — **is** right!

I have used the word **most** to signify the larger part of a group. In ancient Greece, the word **maior** was used to denote a number, not more than half of a greater total, but merely larger than other numbers. In seventeenth century England, the word **majority** was used with the same meaning - a meaning we now give to **plurality**.

Not until Jefferson's *Manual* is there any indication - and even that a rather weak implication in Sections XXVI (26) and XLI (41) - that **majority** means more than half of the total.

Carrying this to its logical extreme, current usage interprets **majority rule** as the rules and customs considered "correct" and "right" by more than one half of the group, society, or nation concerned.

As we examine this in light of our own experiences, many examples will come to mind where what has become legally "right" is not always considered "right" by the majority of the people within a society. In recent days, we have been told that the desecration of the American flag is a right that is guaranteed to us under the First Amendment. Despite this, all evidence seems to indicate that **most** of the people of this nation feel that our flag is a sacred symbol and should be protected.

Faced with this disparity, we often find ourselves listening to a vast variety of propaganda ranging from the shrill and sometimes violent demonstrations of the fanatic fringe to the learned muttering of academics who too frequently believe that their ivory towers accurately reflect reality. Under such circumstances, it becomes difficult indeed to determine which possible solution to a problem would be best for the greatest number — unless it be resolved by a majority vote of those concerned, and then, only when the members of the group are aware of the relevant facts concerning that problem. Their behavioral expectations will have caused the making of rules that will solve the problem.

When the power of any group originates within the group itself, and when that group has developed rules guaranteeing equality and equal rights to all its members, they have adopted democracy as a way of life. The basic principle of democracy is that the voice of the majority will prevail.

This is the blueprint of our temple of parliamentary wisdom and strength. I have placed major emphasis on the Parliamentary Pillars: Ethics, Order, Equality, Justice, and Majority Rule. While I may have written more about one column of the temple than another, it is no indication of relative importance, for each is equal to any other. While any one column might stand alone, it is upon their combined total strength that parliamentary law exists as a powerful protection of democratic government.

COMMITTEES: WHO? WHAT? WHERE? WHEN? WHY?

So much has been said and written about committees that it seems redundant to add more. Yet the questions frequently asked about committee function, composition, and procedure make it obvious that another effort might be appreciated. An appropriate form to present it is suggested by the questions:

Who? What? Where? When? Why?

Starting with the WHO?

A committee is usually formed of a number of members of a group. Rarely, non-members may be asked to do something for the benefit of the insiders, almost always, however, for some type of compensation.

There may be any number of people on a committee. Sometimes just one person is "the committee," sometimes many hundreds. Most committees are small, frequently fewer than ten members. Small committees are concerned with purely local affairs, or with important and extensive planning which will be shared later with the parent organization. Very large committees are usually those with nationwide responsibilities, such as the National Republican or Democratic Committees. Such committees tend to have regional committee members who in turn supervise small local sub-committees working at the "grassroots" level.

When we consider the WHO of committees, it is important to remember that in any organization there are many kinds of people, some eager and enthusiastic, some bored and indifferent, and some genuinely incapable. There have been many things said about the effectiveness of a committee such as "A camel is a horse designed by a committee," but almost always the quality and effectiveness of a committee has been the product of the quality and effectiveness of its members. It was Fred Allen, a famous comedian of the 1930's and 40's, who defined a committee as

"A group of men who individually can do nothing but as a group decide that nothing can be done."

There will always be complaints about committee work, but usually the blame for poor work can be traced to the assigned people who serve (or don't serve) on the committee. Ineffective committee members should be replaced.

WHAT is a committee?

Usually, a committee is a small number of members of an organization united by an assignment or specific goal. They are frequently loosely organized, but with at least two official positions, a chairman and a secretary and, if the committee's task involves funds, a treasurer. Committee members may elect officers although it is traditional that the first person appointed to the committee usually becomes at least the temporary chairman. The chairman of a special committee is almost always the person who saw the need for it and made the motion that such a committee be created. (Obviously the person most interested and, probably, most informed.)

A committee may be permanent in nature or it may be temporary, formed to handle a single action.

Permanent committees, known as "Standing Committees," are usually established in the bylaws. These are the committees upon which the activities of the organization depend. Members assigned to a standing committee usually serve terms concurrent with the terms of the elected officers, but while the members themselves have limited terms, the committee itself continues just as the positions of the elected officers continue after the expiration of their terms. Standing committees are usually responsible for the bylaws, programs, membership and other regularly occurring activities.

Temporary circumstances result in special, or ad hoc committees which are created to accomplish some specific task. The creation of special committees by the president, the board of directors, the entire organization, or a combination of these elements, is usually authorized in the bylaws. The details of duties, responsibilities and membership are developed only when the committee is formed. A special committee reports to whichever authorized officer or group originated it.

Any standing or special committee may be charged with a complex mission and may find that its work may best be done by several sub-committees. In such a case, small groups of members are formed which report to the whole committee, so that a single inclusive report can be made to the appointing authority.

The procedural structure of committees varies greatly depending on its mission, its size, and the personality of its parent organization. It may be strictly business-like, or it may be quite informal. The same parliamentary authority used by its parent usually guides it, but whether that is Robert's *Rules* or some other code, there are several differences in the conduct of business in a meeting. For example, the chairman of a committee may make motions, may speak in discussion without stepping down from the leadership, and he may vote on all questions. Motions don't have to be seconded, there is no limit on the number of times a member may speak, and informal discussion of a proposal is allowed even when no motion is pending.

There are other differences between general assembly procedure and that used by committees according to other authorities:

More freedom of discussion; more time; better use of experts and consultants; delicate questions can be handled without publicity; hearings may be held giving members and outsiders opportunity to express opinions.[22]

Members are not required to obtain the floor and may speak without rising; vote can be taken even if no motion has been made.[23]

Decision made by consensus – no vote is required.[24]

Speakers may speak as many times as they wish if recognized; a motion to reconsider may be offered by any member.[25]

Motions to close or limit debate are not allowed; questions can be raised during a discussion; a vote may be taken without a formal motion when committee members understand a proposal.[26]

WHY is a committee?

Why does an organization need committees? What does a committee do?

There are three different purposes for which a committee may exist. Committees may be created to investigate, to investigate and recommend, or to investigate, recommend, and take action. They may be a permanent element of an organization, or created to confront a temporary situation.

It is a well-established principle of good management that the smallest number of individuals necessary to accomplish a task will be the most efficient number. If you have fewer, either the job will take more time to accomplish or it won't be done at all. If you have more committee members than needed, some of them will do little or nothing and a lot of time will be wasted. It's a simple matter of "Too many cooks spoil the broth."

It was Robert Copeland who wrote, "To get something done, a committee should consist of no more than three people, two of whom are absent."

Obviously, common sense should enter into any committee activity, whether it be just investigating, recommending or actually doing something. Sometimes, faced by a complex problem with many facets, it might be helpful to have a larger number of individual investigators who might be organized into sub-committees. But when the facts have been collected, the chairman of the sub-committee reports to the whole committee which must consider it along with the reports of other sub-committees in order to arrive at the best possible recommendation for presentation to the assembly. When the approved course of action is also the responsibility of the committee, it may again be desirable to have more working committee members.

A committee may be assigned an investigation. When all available information has been acquired, a report must be made to the parent organization. For example, an auditing committee would examine the treasurer's records and report that all was in order.

The initial assignment of a task to a committee may include not only an investigation but also a recommendation. In that case, if an audit committee found discrepancies, its report would recommend possible courses of corrective action.

When a dance committee is formed, it might be required to establish a date, find and hire an appropriate location, procure a band, and get tickets printed and sold as well as a myriad of other tasks. Its report would not be due until the completion of all actions relating to the dance and would summarize all relevant actions and include financial results.

-oOo-

In this brief analysis of the WHO?, WHAT?, and WHY? of committees, I have neglected the WHEN? and WHERE? However, little can be mentioned here of these for obviously circumstances will vary in every instance. A committee functions in accord with the bylaws WHEN and WHERE it can do so conveniently and effectively.

-oOo-

In conclusion, one great truth must be emphasized. The committees of an organization, both the standing committees and any special committees, comprise its working elements. The quality of any organization is significantly dependent upon the strength and effectiveness of its committees and the personnel serving them.

THE POWER OF THE MINORITY

For many years, I have counted myself among the fighters for a more simplified kind of parliamentary practice. For almost as long, I have been, almost single-handed, advocating a procedural code based solely upon the rule of the majority, based upon the decisions made by the major part of the members of any group, organization, or indeed, nation.

The Tenth edition of *Robert's Rules of Order* states that "The basic principle of decision in a deliberative assembly is that, to become the act or choice of the body, a proposition must be adopted by a majority vote; that is, direct approval — implying assumption of responsibility for the act - *must be registered by more than half of the members present and voting on the particular matter*." (page 4) The same authority tells us that modifications of this principle may be required "in the case of certain steps or procedures that impinge on the normal rights of the minority...."

I shall have more to say about those modifications.

Much has been written and said about the very definite responsibility of the majority to protect the rights of the minority. In many articles, I have, as have other writers, spelled out those rights in detail. The rights of the minority include such things as the right to speak for or against a proposal, to remain silent, to vote, to expect courtesy and respect from others, to be nominated and to hold office. But think about this! The minority has also been given, by some parliamentary authorities, the right *and the power* to thwart the will of the majority. This will occur whenever a decision is reached by what is called a super majority vote, that is, a requirement that more than a majority is necessary to decide.

To my knowledge, the first writer to develop in detail the concept that a super majority vote is unfair was Alice Sturgis. In her book, *Learning Parliamentary Procedure*, published in 1953, she wrote:

> Whenever more than a majority vote is required, control passes from the majority to the minority. For example, if a two-thirds vote is required to take an action, one-third of the members make the decision as to whether the measure is to pass or to be lost. Each of the members of the one-third minority, therefore, has twice as much power of decision as each of the members of the majority. Similarly, if a unanimous vote is required, control is taken away from the majority and given to one member.[27]

(Remember the Soviet walk-out and the subsequent unanimous Korean War vote!)

In the new fourth edition of the *Standard Code of Parliamentary Procedure*, Sturgis and the AIP Revision Committee echo her earlier statement.

Riddick and Butcher say much the same:

> Any vote requirement that is greater than a majority is inconsistent with the concept that a majority decides.[28]

While these authorities, and a few others, agree that decision by a super majority is unfair, they have continued to present a number of motions that require a two-thirds majority vote to pass. Sturgis lists only three, the motions to Close Debate, to Limit Debate, and to Suspend the Rules and, sometimes, when used to kill, the motion to Postpone Temporarily. On the other hand, the tinted pages of the latest edition of Robert's *Rules* provide a list of twenty-two motions including ten that require a two-thirds majority under some conditions but not under others.

My own book, *The Majority Rules*, actually crosses the line. As its title suggests, a favorable vote by only one half plus one of those legally entitled to vote who do vote is all that is required in order to pass any motion. But I, too, have left the door open for super majorities. While I have listed none, I believe that any organization which feels a real need for a two-thirds majority vote for matters such as the amendment of bylaws has the authority to create any special motions and any other special rules which may best suit their particular requirements.

But any vote that permits a small group to defeat the will of a larger group is not, in my opinion, a practice consistent with the concept of equality of membership.

However, since many parliamentary authorities endorse the super majority vote, and since some organizations that use my book have made special concessions concerning it, I have been forced to accept this non-democratic practice, but not to approve it.

In these cases, we speak of a practice which has been knowingly accepted by the group, recognizing that under certain conditions to which they subscribe, a minority should have the right to delay or even to prevent a decision favorable to the majority of members.

The concept of Majority Rule has long been recognized as the fundamental principle of democracy — the will of the majority shall govern. Section 508 of Jefferson's *Manual* states, "The voice of the majority decides; for the *lex majoris partis* is the law of all councils, elections, etc., where not otherwise expressly provided." Majority Rule has provided a foundation for our nation and, indeed, for our culture, but its origin is unknown, lost in the dim fog of ancient history.

My idea about that is, I believe, logical enough to be true, even though I cannot prove it with volumes of careful research. I am sure that some ambitious caveman, desiring to be the leader of his tribe, approached a weaker colleague. "Look," he might say while scowling and waving his club, "I am much bigger than you and stronger. Don't you think it would be wise for you to accept me as your leader?" And the idea that power increases in direct relationship to strength would take root.

No, there is nothing new about the slogan, "MIGHT MAKES RIGHT!" History is full of incidents when an issue, a policy, a boundary, and even matters of guilt or innocence have been decided, not by means of an evaluation of information or by a logical development of events, but by the sheer number of participants on one side or the other. Most of the mob, stirred up by self-seeking leaders, called for the release of Barabas, even though Pontius Pilate himself felt that Jesus was innocent. Most of the people of Germany were led to believe that a blond, blue-eyed master race should rule the world and that the eradication of Jews was justified. Time and time again, the world has been torn apart by those who have believed that when one has strength, one is right! When one always has strength, one has the power to be always right.

Page after page could be filled with examples, demonstrating that people tend to cluster around success or a promise of a better life. As a tribal chieftain subdues a rival clan, weaker and defeated members of the enemy will abandon their former leader and thus the size of the winning group, and its consequent power, will increase even further. In this manner, a vast army can be created by the simple act of one man telling another to follow him. A religious leader may build a following as people turn and walk with him, not necessarily because of his physical strength, but possibly his strength of character or because they see in him an opportunity to rise from a bleak and hopeless life to something better.

By definition, a society is a group of human beings broadly distinguished from other groups by mutual interests, by participation in characteristic relationships, by shared institutions and by common culture. Even though the members of that society exist in harmony, every new idea which comes before them will be seen as two-sided, with good features as well as bad. Harmless issues will be easily decided one way or another, but more controversial matters will cause divisive argument which frequently develops into conflict, outright hostility and sometimes violence. While it is true that the society is a group united by common interests, it is not a homogeneous, seamless entity. It is formed of smaller clusters of individuals blended together who share many aspects of life. They may be poor and illiterate or rich and famous. They may be bankers or servants, factory workers or farmers, doctors or carpenters, but they function as a single unit. Almost always, however, within such groups, there exist individuals who want something different, sometimes personal power, sometimes the satisfaction of serving their friends, sometimes a place in history. In our own country, we can look at Thomas Paine and Patrick Henry, John Adams and James Madison, Thomas Jefferson and George Washington, and the other patriots who formed the nucleus which became the Continental Congress and finally the United States of America. It has happened repeatedly throughout history. When the society has become oppressive, some individual rises to meet the occasion. He need not be elected or appointed, he simply emerges from the people and becomes accepted as a leader. Such men frequently meet tragic ends but continue to exist as legends. In England, it was Robin Hood, in Mexico, Emiliano Zapata. The Spanish still revere the man they call El Cid. Che Guevara will live on in Cuba long after Castro's revolution is forgotten, and the name of William Wallace will never die in Scotland.

Other men have stepped out of the ranks to assume positions of leadership. Such a man was Adolph Hitler, who gathered a small group of believers around him. With the power that their unity gave him, he appealed to the strong nationalistic strength of the German people, and threatened the security of our entire world. Such a man was Vladimir Ilyich Lenin, who brought the teachings of Karl Marx to life and plunged an entire nation into seventy-five years of gloom, despair and treachery, a circumstance of doom from which the Russian people are only now emerging. Lenin's Bolsheviks formed only a small minority, but at the first all-Russian Soviet Congress, in June 1917, they easily defeated the much larger but weak and disorganized Kerensky government.

Remember the caveman who enticed a fellow tribesman to follow his leadership and gave birth to the "might is right" theory? Suppose that it didn't happen as I related it, but in this manner. The caveman was hungry and approached his neighbor. "Hey buddy," he might have said, "I'm not big enough or strong enough to kill that juicy mammoth over there alone, but if you will help me, we can both have a fine meal later." And the other might have said, "Sure, I'll help, but let's go after that rhinoceros instead. It can't run so fast and it tastes better." The first caveman might reply, "O.K., but let's get started, I can't stand any more of these raw insects." And, very probably, our two rebels will be joined by others who want some red meat.

When a leader emerges, no matter whether he be a force for good or evil, he advocates a change. He takes a position concerning some issue, usually controversial, which faces the society. While his followers initially form only a small and powerless unit, they may grow in number and strength, and as they do, they will be seen as "rebels" and "misfits." People will begin to fear them for not only will they be "following the beat of a different drummer," but they will be considered, in many instances, to be some kind of threat to the existing way of life. Our caveman hunters might be ostracized and cast out of the tribe, for the majority would prefer the safety of insect-eating to the risks involved with mammoth hunting.

Think of the "rebels" you have encountered or read about. Remember the recording group known as "The Motley Crew" with safety pins thrust through their earlobes and nostrils? Remember the characters you have seen with spiky green hair and clothes so torn and disreputable to be fit only for burning? Remember the painted faces of groups attired like visitors from another planet? We have all seen the "skinheads" of Britain — you can find them here in the United States. And the Neo-Nazis of Germany — we have some of them, too. There are other "hate" organizations in France, in Italy, in Japan, in Korea — And we cannot overlook our own Klu Klux Klan!

These groups, frightening, idiotic or repulsive though they may seem, have their disciples. While we can hope that none of them will cause a world revolution, they are constituted of individuals who have rejected, wholly or in part, the customs, the expected and accepted behaviors and traditions of our culture. They are non-conforming minorities within our society.

But don't condemn them all. Remember that it was a small band of non-conforming rebels who participated in the Boston Tea Party and who defied English law when the Stamp Act threatened "taxation without representation." It was a small group of parliamentarians who assembled around Robert English in 1958 when he rebelled against the restrictions of the National Association of Parliamentarians and founded the American Institute of Parliamentarians.

And each one of these non-conforming minority groups, regardless of orientation, possessed **power**!

Society in America today is formed of roughly 250 million people arranged in a constantly shifting array of groups with loosely established goals. These might range from the replacement of a Democratic politician with a Republican (or vice versa), to other groups who want to change the educational system, to still other groups who want to force South Africa to abolish apartheid. Many millions of these groups overlap, for those who want to crusade against smoking could be in favor of special gay and lesbian rights.

What changes a crowd into a group? It is an objective to work for, a goal which might not be attained by any one individual, but may be reached by people working together, a mutual purpose. And today, in these United States, the crowds of people who make up our population are not unified by any one, single, dominant purpose. We have been, in the past, when the entire nation was unified in the concentration of efforts to win World War II. Now, with no such goal before us, we focus our interests, our time, our energy and our resources on smaller objectives. We join smaller groups, each with its own agenda, each with its own power. And as a national majority, without a sense of direction, without strong leadership and without a major goal, we are beginning to become more and more afraid of the growing powers of the minority groups.

Where does parliamentary procedure fit into all of this? We can turn to our basic parliamentary principles of equality of membership, of freedom of speech, of the protection of rights and the decision by majority rule. We can see that the growth in strength and power of minority groups is not at all consistent with equality, for with an increase in power comes an increase in the potential to use that power. With greater power, a vigorous minority frequently strives to suppress spoken and written opposition. As a minority becomes stronger, the tendency to seek redress, sometimes violently, for real or imagined infringements on personal and group rights and privileges increases. As a minority becomes more powerful, it can become more threatening to others, either because the other groups are satisfied with the *status quo* and don't want it changed, or, more probably, because they are afraid that as one minority becomes more assertive, it will degrade their own position. Initially, however, while the threat is recognized, it is not considered significant, for it consists of a mere minority.

There are, however, many instances where a mere minority becomes significant — when it prevails — not because of a requirement for a super majority vote, but because there is no organized majority. This has happened when there is no commonality upon which the many small groups within an organization can focus and attempt to work together to achieve the group goal. This has happened when there is neither real objective to work toward nor real leadership to point the way toward a solution to whatever obstacle lies before them. That this is true is evidenced in the national election of 1992 when a minority of only 43% elected a president despite the 57% who did not vote for him! That delicate thread of mutual interests and common goals had been dissolved and what had been a majority became, instead, a crowd of individuals and small groups. Such a majority may be classified as one of three types, the *apathetic majority*, the *disorganized majority,* and the *silent majority*.

The *silent majority* was identified by Alice Sturgis who not only defined the term but also wrote more than a page about it and its value. In the past, as a faithful disciple of Alice Sturgis, I have quoted her, I have paraphrased her, and I have agreed totally when she wrote:

> The "silent majority" serves its own important
> purposes. Its members are usually in a better po-
> sition to weigh arguments and make decisions
> than the vocal few; they exercise their own
> highly effective type of eloquence when they
> vote.[29]

Time passes, however, and we read the daily paper with its unending series of stories about small groups of activists who have tumbled vast organizations to the dust — We see one television newscast after another publicizing the havoc and chaos resulting from the actions of small groups of vandals, bigots and misguided fanatics — as I look upon our world today, I see, perhaps more clearly, that the members of the Sturgis "silent majority" are welded into one entity only by the slimmest of bonds — an intelligent appraisal of the facts followed by the "eloquence" of their vote — a bond of unity which is constantly being eroded and weakened by threats, coercion, intimidation, and violence. Of what value is a majority of intelligent members who have carefully evaluated the arguments of "the vocal few," and who

85

fully agree with the proposed course of action towards the desired goal, but who fail to vote because they fear some kind of retribution?

We can find many examples of this. Surely the "silent majority" can be seen in almost every organization — those members who faithfully attend every meeting, pay their annual dues promptly, and vote conscientiously — but rarely participate in discussion or action.

The *apathetic majority* is formed of those who have decided that their opinions and their votes are of little consequence — that whatever will happen will happen regardless of any action they might take. They have convinced themselves that "my single vote can't make any difference, so why vote?" Of what value is a majority of members who know and care very little about group goals and usually cry out and act only after decisions unfavorable to them have been made?

The apathetic majority characterizes a large percentage of the American society, as proven time and time again by our lackluster voter percentage in both local and national elections. I read recently of a major and apparently necessary expenditure of education funds which was defeated, probably resulting in the closure of at least one school — and the matter was decided by votes cast by less than ten percent of the eligible voters!

The *disorganized majority* is composed of groups as well as individual members who may well recognize that conditions must be changed but have no understanding of how to change them nor what they should be changed into. Action among the disorganized majority consists either of mad scrambling or of total immobility.

We see this third type all around us if we really try to determine what is wrong with American life. The disorganized majority is aware that conditions are poor and is anxious to make them better. But they don't know how, and they have no specific goal in view. In desperation, they form small groups behind self-appointed and, in many cases, highly motivated leaders who attempt to use the power of the group to attain what they believe to be the proper goal — a belief not always shared by other leaders. The result is chaos. Only when those minor leaders can find and share a mutual goal can their groups begin to grow together. Only when those minority groups unite behind a common purpose can they become a majority. Only when they put aside their special interests and work together as a single organism can they acquire the power within any social structure to make decisions for that society.

Let us now turn our attention to the parliamentarian and parliamentary procedure. How can we be involved in the power struggle of minority groups, and why should we be concerned with its effect upon society?

The foundation of our America is the belief that the strength of a society originates in the willing sacrifice of personal interests for the good of the community. We firmly believe that the strength of a group is derived from the individuals within it, not from some external source. We believe in equality for all members of our society. We believe in the protection of the rights of all members, whether of the majority or of the minority, and we govern ourselves by the voice of the majority. We know that our society, like any other, cannot exist without order. And we know that all of these things are the tools of the parliamentarian.

In any group, minority or otherwise, the leader's control is on the sharp edge with autocratic dictatorship through over-control on one side and anarchy because of too little control on the other. Parliamentary procedure insists on leadership by consent of the members. By presenting opportunities for the discussion of opposing viewpoints, parliamentary procedure encourages freedom of speech, understanding and compromise rather than intolerance and separation. By insisting on order, parliamentary procedure prevents chaos.

Parliamentary procedure promotes freedom of assembly. A parliamentarian can assist in keeping business focused on the objectives of the organization. A parliamentarian can teach that blatant extremism and terrorism is not an exercise of democratic power, but a demonstration of bigotry and dictatorial arrogance. And more than anything else, a parliamentarian serves to remind everyone that the rights and responsibilities of the majority are also the rights and responsibilities of the minority. Even in a minority group, decisions must be made by majority rule or else the group is controlled by a dictator.

I do not wish to present a gloomy picture of fragmented splinters of our society, existing as minority groups seeking recognition and power in countless and futile efforts to save the world. I do not claim that our unique knowledge of parliamentary wisdom represents the only hope for salvation. But I do want to remind you of the words of Winston Churchill who said,

> Many forms of Government have been tried and will be tried in this world of sin and woe. No one pretends that democracy is perfect or all-wise. Indeed, it has been said that democracy is the worst form of Government except all those other forms that have been tried from time to time.[30]

I believe in parliamentary procedure. I believe that parliamentarians, teachers, consultants, and advisors have a duty to make Churchill's "worst form of government" as understandable and as perfect as it can be. I believe that we must realize that in an organized society, the ideas of even the most powerful and aggressive minority must be respected and considered, not because of intimidating tactics and intolerance of opposing views, but because in any society, the rights, obligations, responsibilities and privileges of all members are equal. Beyond that, the will of the people — the voice of the majority — must decide. I do not believe that a majority decision is always the right decision — nor shall I attempt to convince you that the voice of the majority cannot ever be wrong — But, as Abraham Lincoln asked, "Is there any other better way?"

NAME CHANGE?

In recent years many parliamentary writers have been concerned with the lack of popularity of classes in procedure at schools, colleges and even within adult groups, many of which usually have inadequate parliamentary leadership. One reason, it has been frequently suggested, is the frightening formality of the term "parliamentary procedure."

More than one writer has recommended a change. Several years ago, Roberta McDow, a delightful writer, asked, *What's In A Name?* She presented some very cogent arguments in favor of a change in terminology, advocating the use of the term "democratic procedure."[31]

This is a change, which, I believe, is long overdue. Thousands of organizational members have remained a considerable distance from parliamentary procedure simply because the name itself was intimidating and their past experience with it had been both chaotic and frustrating. Many parliamentarians are endeavoring to convince people that what we teach is a simple, easily understood method for maintaining order in a meeting.

McDow's article stopped short of demanding that we install her substitution. She merely suggested that parliamentary teachers make certain that students of parliamentary procedure understand that what they are learning is actually democratic procedure.

I would vote for that with enthusiasm. But as I contemplate the total picture, I'm not sure that I would endorse any further replacement. We would encounter some difficult problems were we to do so. And I have no solutions to suggest.

For example, what would we call ourselves? If not "parliamentarians," would we be "democritians" or "democrits"? Surely not "democrats"! I would have no difficulty writing about the techniques of democracy nor in discussing a democratic procedure. But I am not at all sure that I would become a member of the National Association of Demopros or of the American Institute of Democracities.

What's in a name? Actually, a great deal rides on the name we call ourselves. I take pride in being known in my community as a parliamentarian, even though more than one person, after congratulating me on being one, has asked me just what do I do when I am being a parliamentarian. I'm not sure that I would be as well known were I called by another name.

All of this has caused another thought to arise. We have an unusual collection of collective nouns for various groups of creatures. We talk about a "pride of lions," "a herd of cattle," " a flock of sheep" (for some reason, we seem to have classified sheep as some kind of bird.) Speaking of birds, did you know that a group of meadow larks is called an "exaltation"? A "gaggle" of geese is a group of geese floating around on the lake, but if they are flying around in that familiar V-shape, it is a "skein" of geese! How about a "communion" of Christians? You may have known that a "covey" of partridges is correct, but did you know that a covey is limited to just a family? If it is a group, larger than a family, you are supposed to call it a "pack."

There are many more of these special terms, but my research has yielded nothing to describe a gathering of parliamentarians. If we were to call ourselves "democraticians" or some such label, we should pay some heed to whatever collective noun is used to describe a group of us.

This is a matter to which I have devoted considerable thought. I thought that we might properly use a "convention" of parliamentarians, but that is not sufficiently exclusive. A "discussion" could be used, but that would suit many other groups as well as our own. Frankly, I cogitated about this for a long time without success, but spurred by my reading of "What's In A Name?" I felt that if the time is ripe for a modification in nomenclature, it also might be the right time to propose an appropriate collective term for a group of parliamentarians.

Based upon years of experience at many conventions, parliamentary and otherwise, I now place before you my recommendations:

Henceforth, whenever three or more parliamentarians are gathered together, let the group be known to all as a **"CHALLENGE!"**

However, when parliamentarians are assembled as a large, formal and organized group, the use of the term "challenge" might be considered appropriate, but my past experience says otherwise. "Challenge" would be as inadequate as "moist and good-sized" would be in describing the Pacific Ocean. Some parliamentary conventions have exposed hidden interests and have resulted in great divisiveness. I feel that under such circumstances, the term **"CLEAVAGE"** would be in order. We could say, for example, that "the cleavage of parliamentarians was very obvious as the arguments for and against the controversial motion became more hostile."

In all seriousness, I want to enthusiastically endorse the proposal made by Roberta McDow. Call it what we may, parliamentary procedure *is* democratic procedure. Why not give students the knowledge that what they are learning is a system that protects our American way of life, not a complex and mysterious set of rules and traditions without any practical application.

MINORITY POWER HAS TAKEN CONTROL!

There will be many who scoff at this title. There will be many who will agree that we have concentrated so much on the significance of the rights of the minority that the rights of the majority have become relatively insignificant. Few, however, will agree with the title of this article. Most will argue that never, at least never in these United States, would we ever allow ourselves to be controlled by the power of the minority!

NO?

Let's look back a few years. In the 1968 presidential election, nearly seventy-three million voters cast ballots. If we consider the popular vote, disregarding the Electoral College, a candidate would have had to garner about 37 million votes to be elected. As it was, no candidate had more than 32 million. Richard Nixon was elected by a minority and it was a smaller minority of 10 million votes for George Wallace that controlled the election. In 1992, Bill Clinton received 43 million, seven hundred thousand votes. George Bush had 38 million. If either candidate had been able to claim the nearly twenty million votes cast for Ross Perot, we would have had a president with a "mandate from the majority." As it is, however, of the more than one hundred million citizens who voted, almost sixty million voted for a candidate other than Bill Clinton. That means that sixty percent of the vote was cast for somebody else — not the winner!

The relatively small group who voted for Perot controlled the election.

It is becoming more and more obvious that majority decisions are significantly dependent upon several factors:

- A majority must be a cohesive entity;

- A majority must have a specific goal;

- A majority must be informed; and

- A majority must never underestimate the power of the minority

and probably most important of all:

- A majority must recognize that it may be wrong!

A Cohesive Majority

Years ago, I thought I invented, as a mere rhetorical device, a theory which claimed that there was no such thing as a majority. There were, I said, only innumerable groups of minorities temporarily united for mutual and self-serving goals. Little did I realize at that time that my theory was true. Every majority is really a group of separate entities which cohere to other similar groups only until certain individual goals have been attained, after which the majority dissolves.

If we accept this as true, we can postulate that majorities can exist only when some mutual objective holds the individual elements together in sufficient number to acquire power. We can be grateful that many small groups have not succeeded in developing into a majority because their goals are not sufficiently universal to be shared by other small groups. We can look no further than the Klu Klux Klan for such an example. Many of today's fringe fanatics and gangs advocate violence against our culture but they remain impotent because there is at this time no cohesive objective which might bind them together. Those of us who prefer the status quo must not forget that those small minority groups can, and frequently do, prevent the formation of a majority decision. For the majority to decide anything, the many different unities within it must adhere to an objective which is recognized as an attainable goal which is of mutual advantage.

A Specific Goal

In the same vein, the strength of a majority is proportional to the preciseness of its goals. A vague and indefinite purpose serves only to bring individuals together and cannot produce a group which will work in unity to attain some real objective. Most people are opposed to "sin", but until it is clear to them exactly what the term means, very few will take any action to eliminate it The groups which presently oppose or support the abortion issue must each develop a precise statement of purpose and philosophy. When and if that happens, today's conflict over the issue may be resolved. There are militant groups who profess a hatred of the present American government. They are articulate and vigorous but their common link — hatred of the government — is still too general to become a rallying cry for a majority. But it is easily possible that a number of such groups of individuals, unified by a clearly defined purpose but yet not equal in number to those opposed to that purpose, will prevail because the opposition itself is frequently apathetic because its goal is vague and uncertain.

An Informed Majority

I have been more vocal than most parliamentarians in espousing the philosophy that "the voice of the people should decide." Much that I have written centers on the fact that an expression of approval of a proposition by more than one half of a group should be adequate for the decision-making process. But I firmly believe that a majority vote should be the basis for parliamentary decision making *provided that adequate information and appropriate time for its evaluation are available.*

If we can trust the majority to make wise decisions, we must also trust it to acknowledge the availability or lack of time and facts. Majority decisions can be wrong, as countless jury trials will attest. But the errors made by majority decisions diminish in number as the accuracy and the completeness of available information increases.

In a letter to the citizens of Albemarle dated February 12, 1790, Thomas Jefferson wrote:

> ...the will of the majority, the NaturalI law of every society, is the only sure guardian of the rights of man. Perhaps even this may sometimes err. But its errors are honest, solitary and short-lived. --Let us then, my dear friends, forever bow down to the general reason of the society. We are safe with that, even in its deviations, for it soon returns again to the right way.[32]

It is obviously essential that a majority decision be founded upon as many of the facts available as possible. To base a decision upon self-interest, passion or misguided enthusiasm is to generate dissension, distrust and eventual disorder.

Recognition of Minority Power

There are no problems for majority power more significant than ignorance, apathy, complacency, and over-confidence. No matter how large the numerical strength of a majority may be, a small but unified and aggressive minority can seize power without difficulty. In Russia, in 1918, the October Revolution of the Bolsheviks enabled a group of fewer than a thousand to take over Russia. Hitler's Brown Shirts made up an extremely small minority group but public apathy combined with ignorance of Hitler's goals enabled him to grasp power from the majority. When a majority doesn't know what the minority's purposes are, or doesn't care, it is in danger. When a majority believes that a minority is harmless and totally without power, it is in danger. When a candidate for political office feels that his opponent "can't possibly win", he is in danger. A winner must never underestimate the opposition.

Acceptance of Error

In a democracy, we have accepted decision by majority vote as the best solution to the problem of governance. I hope that the preceding paragraphs have shown that majority power is a product of united acceptance of a mutual goal, of knowledge about the issue, and of a desire for action. What has not yet been addressed is the question of tolerance of other viewpoints.

If the majority of the members of a group formulate a specific course leading toward the attainment of a goal, it is probable that they will succeed in reaching it — provided they maintain an adequate flexibility, a willingness to listen to other possible means of action and to compromise when the minority suggests something more expeditious. Most of all, a majority must be able to admit an error and to correct it when possible. A majority can be wrong.

I am in full agreement with Thomas Jefferson's statement that decision by majority vote is an essential element of democracy. I am also aware of Henrik Ibsen's terrible indictment of the majority in Act Four of his play, "An Enemy of the People":

> The majority never has right on its side. Never, I say! That is one of the social lies that a free, thinking man is bound to rebel against. What makes up the majority in any given country? Is it the wise men or the fools? I think we must agree that the fools are in a terrible, over-whelming majority, all the wide world over.

In *Huckleberry Finn*, Mark Twain wrote, "Hain't we got all the fools in town on our side? And ain't that a big enough majority in any town?"

However, in his book, *First Principles*, Herbert Spencer wrote:

> The fact disclosed by a survey of the past that majorities have been wrong must not blind us to the complementary fact that majorities have usually not been entirely wrong.

Even a casual survey of history will disclose numerous instances where the decision of a majority has been wrong, not the least of which was the pardon of Barabbas. Even the insistence that a jury of twelve must make a unanimous decision (a 100% majority vote!) has not insured that every person convicted was guilty.

I firmly believe that majority rule must be the basis of any *informed* decision and, indeed, is the very foundation of real democracy.

EQUALITY, FAIRNESS AND COMMON SENSE

Years ago, I wrote a book, *The Majority Rules*.

My purpose was to establish a modified system of procedure based upon generally accepted parliamentary principles, but which stressed simplicity and popular usage. *The Majority Rules* has attained moderate success and is currently in use by a number of schools and colleges for basic instruction and by church, civic and other groups as their parliamentary authority.

The themes, which are emphasized throughout the book, are **equality**, **fairness** and **common sense**.

We are currently embroiled in national events in which divergent paths lie before us, each one of which is pointed out to us as "the only way to go." I find myself wishing that, somehow, my advocacy of equality, fairness and common sense could be applied, not only to parliamentary situations, but also to our entire culture.

Surely there can be no argument about EQUALITY. Slavery existed in our nation when the Declaration of Independence asserted that "all men are created equal," but it took almost ninety years for that statement to begin to grow into Lincoln's Emancipation Proclamation and the Thirteenth Amendment. Equality did not come easily, even then. Most of the country refused to allow women to vote. The Nineteenth Amendment was ratified in 1920. Equal rights legislation has become frequent during the past forty years, but real equality is still a much-sought-after goal.

In our culture, we have learned to insist on our individual personal rights. However, in many cases we have willingly surrendered a small portion of those rights in the name of law and order. Everyone has equal rights, but we have voluntarily allowed ourselves to be equally controlled by rules that prohibit the exercise of one person's rights from infringing on the rights of others. In our democratic republic, every adult citizen has an equal right to vote and that vote counts no more nor less than the vote of any other citizen.

A glaring example of an exception to this is the device found in many parliamentary rules that prescribe a two-thirds majority for certain actions. Most people who insist on this do not realize that with the implementation of this rule, a minority vote is more powerful than a majority vote. In a group of one hundred, a sixty-six-vote majority would lose to a thirty-four-vote minority. While the rights of a minority must be protected, decisions should reflect the will of the majority, and would do so if we can ever attain real equality.

As a nation, we have allowed ourselves to forget that equality applies to responsibilities and rights as well as to opportunities and salaries.

FAIRNESS is a concept that everyone knows but few respect. In recent years, the term "a level playing field" has become part of the popular vocabulary. No one wants to play the game with loaded dice or inferior equipment. But instead of working to acquire skills and working toward a better education, much effort is expended in looking for the "gimmick," the loophole, the extra advantage. Fairness exists only when everyone has the same kind of opportunity. Without fairness, our civilization would deteriorate into total chaos and no one would ever be able to play on a level field.

Turning once again to the field of parliamentary law, we find that most of the traditional authorities are adamant in their belief that only those individuals who voted with the majority in favor of a proposal may request that any decision reached be discussed further prior to implementation, possibly upon acquisition of additional information. Despite the fact that all members are considered equal, anyone who voted against the proposal automatically forfeited the right to move for "reconsideration." This is unfair to a minority member, yet is considered correct procedure according to traditional parliamentary rules.

The role of COMMON SENSE, the most important element of the parliamentary philosophy I advocate, should require no further explanation. But perhaps a few examples will show why I feel so strongly about its paramount significance.

The rule says that there shall be no sexual harassment by and among students – a six-year-old boy was suspended from first grade for kissing a girl on the cheek at her request. What about common sense?

The rule says that there will be no drug traffic in the school — a fourteen-year-old honor student was suspended for three months because she gave her girl friend a Midol tablet. What about common sense?

It was a meeting of parents and teachers, assembled to make some plans for recognition for those who had contributed hours to a local program called "Reading Excitement." Voluntary time spent with first, second and third grade students had begun to pay off, for more children were appearing at the school library to borrow books.

Ruth had an idea. "How about a prize for the child who reads the most books from now until the end of school?" she asked.

Mary responded, "I think it would be better to reward the volunteer who inspired that child."

The rules say that a proposal for action at a meeting should be made in the form of a motion and be properly seconded. They also say that an amendment to change the first proposal should also be made as a motion and be properly seconded. In their discussion, these women may produce an excellent, constructive plan that should prove a fine incentive to a needed volunteer service. But what about the rules? There were no motions and no seconds – only proposals which may lead to an agreement. What about common sense?

EQUALITY, FAIRNESS and COMMON SENSE are too frequently ignored because of "the rules." Rules and law are the bases upon which our culture is established. Without some kind of regulation, only chaos can result. Yet a blind adherence to the rules will prohibit personal initiative and stifle both intellectual and economic growth.

In too many instances a well-intentioned law becomes enveloped in complex interpretations which appear to exist only to victimize us. We must learn to temper such laws with common sense just as we need to examine them for fairness and equality.

Many will disagree. Many will argue that we must have specific rules to guide us and keep us from destroying ourselves. They feel that without detailed rules, we would not know what to do. I agree that we need rules, we need guidance, we need some kind of structure so that we may progress with fairness for all from Point A to Point B – and beyond. It has been said that when a well-known parliamentary authority believed that when an event occurred which was not covered by a rule, he should (and did) write a new rule. This practice is not limited to parliamentarians for it can be seen frequently in the legislative halls of our nation. Unfortunately, new situations constantly arise and unless someone applies common sense, we shall inevitably be buried beneath mountains of legality. Instead of writing new laws, we should base our actions more on a better application of existing rules combined with common sense.

Many times, meetings are interrupted when a member becomes insistent upon a very precise wording of a motion. There have been such cases when the motion itself was out of order!

Sometimes the rules are being adhered to so rigidly that there is no room for common sense. If we are really concerned with "the harmonious transaction of business," no business meeting should be transformed into a parliamentary procedure classroom.

If we could refuse to be restricted by arbitrary rules and dictatorial regulations written by people unfamiliar with the circumstances; if we could allow ourselves to be guided by equality, fairness and common sense, our world would be freed from petty lawsuits, unfriendly neighborhoods and excessive, costly paperwork.

Perhaps it would be a better world.

SEX AND VIOLENCE

They told me that no book can be successful without some sex and violence.

Well, here they are..

Normally, there is not, nor should there be a place for sex and violence in parliamentary procedure. But we must recognize that parliamentary procedure is a system for reaching group decisions, and far too frequently, group decision-making involves violence. For example, a quick look at our American history shows much uncontrolled parliamentary hostility concerning

- ALCOHOL – The Eighteenth Amendment to our Constitution prohibited the manufacture, sale, import or export of intoxicating liquors. But smuggling and illicit manufacture of "bootleg" liquor could not be prevented and much illegal drinking and lawlessness prevailed. Murder and gang action were accepted methods of decision making. Carrie Nation took her axe into the saloons and bars to cast her vote with violence. Al Capone registered his disagreement with the law with machine guns.

- CIVIL RIGHTS - Equal rights for women? Equal rights for slaves? These were questions which faced the founding fathers in the 1790's, and which in many forms face us today. Unrestrained violence is less common now, but the Ku-Klux Klan was a political party that cast its votes with burning crosses.

- ABORTION - Surely no one can forget that only a few years ago, there were strikes, demonstrations and even murder because some people failed to accept a political decision.

These examples, however, were not actually parliamentary but rather the result of parliamentary action. In most cases they were mob actions, not within a parliamentary legislature. But the legislature itself is not immune. According to the *Congressional Research Service,* Sam Houston, at that time a Tennessee Representative, attacked Ohio Representative William Stanbery with his cane when there was disagreement about a vote. A few Years later, Kentucky Representative William J. Graves killed Representative Jonathan Cilley of Maine in a duel, an action which caused Congress to ban duels in the District of Columbia. Abolitionist Charles Sumner's notable antislavery speech in 1856 so angered Preston Brooks, a representative from South Carolina, that he entered the Senate chamber and bludgeoned Sumner with a cane. Brooks later resigned while Sumner needed three years to recover from the beating. There have been other incidents. While we have not heard about physical violence within the Congress in recent years, there can be no question that verbal violence abounds. In 2003, police were called to a House committee meeting after a verbal spat between Representatives Scott McInnes of Colorado and Pete Stark of California, during which Stark is said to have dared McInnes to fight after calling him a "little fruitcake."

Personally, I have witnessed but one instance where violence occurred. It was in a small town meeting where allocations of federal funds were being decided. One member of the committee made a motion, which was seconded, only to inspire considerable and sometimes bitter argument. Eventually, a vote was taken and only one vote was cast in favor of the motion (by the proposer, of course). The man who had seconded it had either voted against it or abstained, which he had a perfectly legal right to do. It was quite a shock, especially to the seconder, when the original proposer of the motion left his seat, marched across the room and struck the seconder squarely in the face.

Yes, there are many examples of the intrusion of physical and, even worse, verbal violence into the world of parliamentary procedure. To expand further on the subject is not my purpose here. I must point out, however, that it has been clearly demonstrated that parliamentary violence does exist but should not be tolerated. Group decision-making is best served in a calm and logical atmosphere in which emotional outbursts can be restricted.

But what about sex?

Just as violence can be seen in parliamentary activity, there are many instances where we can see examples of parliamentary sex!

PARLIAMENTARY SEX? — Surely I jest!

No, it's true. The parliamentary vocabulary is innocent, but the "politically correct" attitude of some participants has brought about the virtual elimination of a key parliamentary term due to the influence of sexism. We have used the term "mankind" for many years to denote the species known as homo sapiens, meaning modern people. The word "human" applied to all of us. Today, it seems, the three letters spelling "man," now indicate only those of us who are male. Female activists are vigorously applying pressure to eliminate any other meaning. (There may be some problem, yet unsolved, with the word "woman.")

As far as I know, no actual physical violence has occurred, but more than one organization has been profoundly disturbed by emotional outbursts.

In days of old, positions of authority were filled by leaders like King Arthur. Even at the Round Table, according to legend, he sat in a prominent throne, or chair. The leaders became known as "chairmen," not because they were men, but because they were people of authority who happened to be male. Today, we have thousands of organizations that are guided by men and women who have been chosen by their peers because of their abilities rather than by their sex. But we hesitate when we address them.

Do we use the title "Chairman" and ignore the problem even when the leader is obviously female, or do we resort to "Madam Chairman?" or the clumsy "Madam (or Mister) Chairperson?" There is no difficulty when we speak to the "President." for this term is without any sexual connotations. But in writing, the leadership position frequently becomes "the chair," or "the presiding officer" and even "the presider." When speaking about, but not directly to him (or her), one could say that "the Chair recognized the speaker," but I have never heard the "chair" addressed as such. Were I a presiding officer, there are many titles I would prefer rather than be called a 'Chair." It was perfectly proper to call on "Mr. Chairman," but who would want to be addressed as either Mr. or Madam Chair?

I cannot foresee the final outcome of this conflict. Perhaps the term "chairman" will vanish forever — maybe some new title will be invented and become popular — possibly organizations will be presided over by "Chiefs" or "Captains."

It is also very likely that all of this will be forgotten.

Regardless of what may happen in the future, it remains my personal conviction that while both violence and sex will be found in parliamentary situations, they serve only to contaminate the courteous, tactful and logical actions of good parliamentary procedure.

PARLIAMENTARY SIMPLICITY

I like to feel that I am following in the footsteps of General Henry Martyn Robert. The last years of his life were devoted to making a difficult and sometimes frustrating system of decision-making procedures understandable and useful. I am an advocate of parliamentary simplicity.

It is important that you understand what I mean by "parliamentary simplicity." It is a term with both favorable and unfavorable meanings, depending upon one's point of view. Remember the politician seeking re-election who was asked to explain his attitude toward WHISKEY.

"My position," he said, "concerning whiskey is perfectly clear. If by 'whiskey' you mean that vile concoction that drags man to the lowest depths of degradation; that despoiler of mind and body; that foul and frightful fluid that corrupts and destroys whatever it touches and leads all mankind to depravity and sin; that destroyer of family and friend; that gateway to the beggar's grave – if that is what you mean by 'whiskey,' then rest assured that I am totally and unalterably opposed to it in any form.

"But," he continued, "if by 'whiskey' you mean that golden elixir which has inspired men to unlimited creativity; that pure and wholesome beverage that permits us to dream the impossible dream and attain the unattainable; if by 'whiskey' you mean that concoction of inspiration and perspicacity which has opened doors to success and profit; that luminous liquid which has transformed strangers into friends and changed despair into courage and hope; if that is what you mean by 'whiskey,' then know that it is dear to my heart and I embrace it with all my soul and body."

To paraphrase that unknown politician, may I say that what I mean by "parliamentary simplicity" is the elimination of confusion; the reduction of anachronisms and redundancies; the proscribing of outmoded and mystical language and ritual; the re-establishment of parliamentary procedure as a tool for all to use in the efficient and harmonious transaction of business, then I am totally and unalterably committed to its development and ultimate success.

Please do not misunderstand me. I have great respect for the fundamental principles of parliamentary law which are rooted in history, Americanized by Thomas Jefferson and Luther Cushing and popularized by Henry Robert. Those principles are as valid today as they were in the past and no advocate of simplification would (or could) alter them. We can read them in every parliamentary text:

- Parliamentary procedure exists to promote the harmonious and cooperative transaction of business.

- All members of a group have equal rights, privileges and obligations.

- The will of the majority is the will of the group.

- The rights of the minority must be safeguarded.

- Free and equal opportunity for discussion and participation is guaranteed.

- Discussion and debate is limited to one subject at a time.

- Equal courtesy and justice for all members is guaranteed.

General Robert had a dream described in the introductory pages of nearly every edition of the *Rules of Order*. He found through considerable personal experience that many different interpretations of the rules of the United States Senate and House of Representatives were being used as procedural guides by various decision-making bodies. Cushing's *Manual* contributed additional versions with the result that nowhere was there any consistency in the conduct of meetings. Robert had a vision of a system of parliamentary procedure which would provide a uniform code for all voluntary groups, thus enabling a member of one to function easily in another.

In the preface to the 1970 edition of the *Rules of Order*, Sarah Corbin Robert wrote of her father-in-law,

> He believed that for achievement of the full measure of the democratic process, a familiarity with the basic provisions of a single, adequate manual should become the common property of all persons engaged in organization work.

Robert felt that despite any differences in location, membership or purpose, every organization would be controlled by identical procedural rules. To transfer such a vision into reality was his challenge, and General Robert rose to meet it. His *Pocket Manual of Order for Deliberative Assemblies* provided a uniform code of procedure which, with subsequent editions, might well have accomplished his purpose. In fact, we have no reason to believe that it did not. More recently, however, Robert's *Rules of Order*, despite its immense popularity, has failed its originator's dream. Uniformity of parliamentary procedure does not exist in the United States. The fault, however, lies only partly with his book; probably much more blame can be placed upon the very people for whom it was created.

Many of us are familiar with people who own vast libraries of unread books. It is not uncommon to see students laden with backpacks overflowing with books they don't have time to read. To some people, the possession of books is the equivalent to the possession of knowledge.

It is a frequently repeated statement that within the United States, the Bible is the only non-fiction book which has outsold Robert's *Rules of Order*. That may be true or not, but everyone reading these words is well aware that few people who own Robert's *Rules* have read it, and of these few, only a very small minority understands it. This explains why, in our culture, a place exists for trained parliamentarians and parliamentary consultants.

But trained parliamentarians and consultants are far from unified and many do not agree with the vision of General Robert. Because of this disagreement, two major points of view have developed. Many experts adhere to one which firmly asserts that excellent and very adequate rules now exist – the challenge is to educate people to use these rules properly. The second believes with equal conviction that as long as people and their organizations exist in different forms, their rules and interpretations of rules will differ. Simply put, this second group prefers to make the rules fit the people rather than trying to make the people fit the rules.

Robert's *Rules of Order*, and there are other established codes of procedure, provides us with a smooth, easy pathway to proceed to our objective with few obstacles – provided we can be taught to use them properly. Many groups and organizations know of the existence of Robert's *Rules*, but find it convenient to make their own path toward their objective. Their bylaws may state that Robert is their parliamentary authority, but the minutes of their meetings attest to their acceptance of other, more convenient rules. No matter what manual or code is mentioned in the bylaws, the actual procedure used in the average voluntary club, society or organization deviates so much from their official parliamentary guide that it becomes something totally new and different.

There is nothing wrong with that. Every organization is a unique entity, entirely individualized by purpose, geography, local economic conditions, and by the personalities who make up its membership. Even separate chapters of large organizations tend to operate differently, even though bound together by common objectives and bylaws. In many cases, the local unit has created its own set of procedures because it was easier, more convenient or because the existing rules didn't quite fit the circumstances.

Many of these groups are ranchers, farmers, parent-teacher associations, welfare workers and just plain common folk who have littler time to accomplish what they want to do and far less time to learn complex procedures and rules that never quite seem to fit the situations facing them. They want to accomplish the business of their organization as quickly and efficiently as possible, yet they don't want or do they have the time for any parliamentary instruction on how to do it.

There is a story told that when the campus of a certain mid-western college was designed, all of the buildings were placed in appropriate places. Then the landscape planners began to put in sidewalks between the buildings, but were stopped by the architect. "The students," he said, "will tell us where to place the pathways."

In parliamentary procedure, parliamentary authorities such as General Henry Robert, George Demeter, Alice Sturgis and others have established "sidewalks." Many groups have adopted these as authorized rules for attaining the objectives of the group. More than one of those groups, however, rebel against a rigid adherence to these rules, despite adopting them. The members prefer a more relaxed and informal approach. Instead of standing to obtain recognition as prescribed, many organizations permit asking for the floor by waving one's hand in the air. Instead of referring to other members as "Mr. Smith" or "Miss Jones," they may speak of "Bill" or "Mary."

Such organizations are designing their own pathways, their own rules. Almost invariably, this results in parliamentary simplification.

No reason exists why groups cannot make their own rules. The only restrictions are that whatever rules exist must be applied equally to all members and that all members must agree to them.

What is wrong with the existing rules? Why should groups adopt the parliamentary codes written by authorities and then change them? There are several reasons. Probably the most significant is that many existing rules are presented in obscure and confusing language. For example, why should there be a motion to "Move the Previous Question?" Presiding officers have been known to ask what question is referred to. The motion to "Adjourn to an Adjourned Meeting" is equally confusing.

There can be no problem when, in large assemblies such as national political conventions, a high degree of formality is required. Decorum assists in the control of the members and inappropriate behavior affects effectiveness. This is equally true with small groups, but informality can be encouraged. Why have a rule requiring a speaker to stand when everyone present can both hear and see him? Why have a rule requiring speakers to limit their words to ten minutes when no one in the group ever speaks for more than two? If business can be accomplished in an atmosphere of simple, relaxed informality, nothing can be gained by enforcing stifling rules.

A third reason for simplification can be seen in procedures that have become almost ludicrous because of redundancy or complexity. When a "Committee of the Whole" makes a decision, it then reports to the main assembly – comprised of exactly the same people who made the decision as a committee ten minutes earlier.

Parliamentary simplicity means a set of rules that can be easily understood and used by all members of a society. Parliamentary simplicity means that obscure language and complex procedures are eliminated. Parliamentary simplicity means that business can be conducted efficiently and effectively without recourse to special training and expert opinion of outsiders.

Henry Robert's vision – to provide a universal code of procedure that could be used and understood by everyone – came at least partly true. His *Rules of Order* was suitable in style and language for the customs that existed at that time. He combined a number of confusing parliamentary systems into a useful and understandable tool. He brought parliamentary procedure up-to-date.

This is my vision, too, By means of the essays in this little book, I hope that I have demonstrated that parliamentary procedure can be appropriate to the hurried yet casual and informal tempo of modern life. I hope that I have shown that parliamentary procedure can be both simple and effective.

AFTERTHOUGHT

In the hope that this book has introduced you to a new appreciation of parliamentary procedure, I want to call your attention to these ideas:

The primary concern of parliamentary procedure is to expedite the harmonious transaction of business by means of tact, courtesy and common sense.

FUNDAMENTALS OF PARLIAMENTARY PROCEDURE

- Everyone is equal, with equal rights and opportunities.
- Every proposal is made in good faith for the good of the group, is free of trickery, and is as clearly worded and simple as possible.
- Only one person may speak at a time.
- Only one subject may be spoken about at a time.
- Minority rights must be protected.
- Majority rights must be accepted by all members of the group.

AND

Don't forget Farwell's "Rule of Parliamentary Simplicity":

Don't have a rule unless you need it; if you need it, use it consistently.

ABOUT THE AUTHOR

Hermon W. ("Hy") Farwell (Columbia University, B.A.,1940, The Pensylvania State University, M.A. 1964) retired from the United States Air Force to enter teaching at Southern Colorado State College (now Colorado State University – Pueblo). Early in his academic career, he was drafted as the parliamentarian of the faculty senate and immediately realized that he needed to know more about the subject. He established credentials as a certified parliamentarian in 1967, and has since been involved as a teacher, a convention speaker, an editor and a practicing parliamentarian. He has written a book, *The Majority Rules* and several brief pocket guides which have been very successful, as well as innumerable articles, many of which have found a place in this book.

Today, semi-retired, he spends most of his spare time in writing, consultations, and in efforts to learn more about his computer.

COMMENTS

The original material from which this book is drawn consists of convention speeches, magazine articles, and class lectures written during a span of nearly forty years. Most of them were originally published in the pages of *The Parliamentary Journal*, the quarterly publication of the American Institute of Parliamentarians, to which I express my appreciation for the opportunity to collect and republish them in this form.

BIBLIOGRAPHY

Anyone desiring more specific parliamentary texts for study and reference should consult any (or all) of the following. While Robert's *Rules of Order Revised* and *The Standard Code* by Sturgis are most widely used, the others listed are competent but of varying degrees of complexity. As a parliamentary authority for an organization, you should select one which best fills your need.

Cannon, Hugh, *Canon's Concise Guide to Rules of Order*, Houghton Mifflin, Boston, 1992.

Demeter, George, *Demeter's Manual of Parliamentary Law and Procedure,* Little Brown and Co., Boston, 1969.

Deschler, Lewis, *Deschler's Rules of Order*, Prentice-Hall, Inc., Englewood Cliffs, New Jersey, 1976.

Ericson, Jon L., *Notes and Comments on Robert's Rules, Revised Edition*, Southern Illinois University Press, Carbondale, 1991

Farwell, Hermon W., *The Majority Rules*, 2nd Edition, High Publishers, Pueblo, Colorado, 1988.

Hills, George S., *Managing Corporate Meetings*, The Ronald Press, New York, 1977

Keesey, Ray E., *Modern Parliamentary Procedure*, Houghton Mifflin, Boston, 1974.

Mason, Paul, *Manual of Legislative Procedure*, The Senate, California Legislature, 1979

Patnode, Darwin, *A History of Parliamentary Procedure*, 3rd. Edition, Parliamentary Publishing, Minneapolis, 1982.

Sturgis, Alice, *The Standard Book of Parliamentary Procedure*, 4th Edition, Revised by the American Institute of Parliamentarians, McGraw-Hill, New York, 2001.

Sturgis, Alice F. *Learning Parliamentary Procedure*, McGraw-Hill Book Company, New York, 1953

Riddick, Floyd M. and Miriam H. Butcher, *Riddick's Rules of Procedure*, Charles Scribner's Sons, New York, 1985.

Riddick, Floyd M., *Senate Procedure*, United States Government Printing Office, 1981

Robert, Henry M., *Robert's Rules of Order Newly Revised*, 10th Edition, Perseus Publishing, Cambridge, Massachusetts, 2000.

Welty, Joel David, *Welty's Book of Procedure*, Caroline House Publishers, Inc, Aurora, IL 1982

ENDNOTES

1   When I wrote "A New Quorum Requirement", I thought I had invented something new. It was a letter from James Lochrie, of Toronto, Canada, a former president of the American Institute of Parliamentarians, which told me how wrong I was. The concept of the "majority of the quorum" was hardly new. Not only did some organizations in California use this to avoid members walking out of a meeting to break the quorum, the idea is mentioned in the records of the Government of Pennsylvania in 1683. I have also found mention of the idea of the majority of the quorum in Sturgis, Learning Parliamentary Procedure.

2   Edmund Randolph, quoted in Peters, William, *A More Perfect Union*, Crown Publishers, New York, 1987, page 137

3   Benjamin Franklin, quoted in Peters, William, *A More Perfect Union*, Crown Publishers, New York, 1987, pages 210-211.

4   William O.Douglas, quoted in Sturgis, Alice, *The Standard Code*, page 1.

5   Robert, page34.

6   Cannon, page 101

7   Robert, page35

8   Keesey, page 31

9   Riddick, page 158

10   A second of angular measurement is equal to 1/60th of a minute of arc, and also of a minute of latitude when measured at the equator and equals approximately 6076 feet, commonly known as a nautical mile. A speed of one nautical mile an hour is called a knot. Not every parliamentarian knows that.

11   Robert, page 259

12   Sturgis, page 86

13   Sturgis, *Learning*, page319

14   Sturgis, page 124

15   Hills, page 341

16   Robert, page 4

17   Mason, pages 73-74

18   Deschler, page 213

19   Robert, page 388

20 Riddick, *Senate*, pages 228-229

21 Thomas Jefferson, in a letter to Baron von Humboldt in 1817, quoted in Sturgis, page 123

22 Sturgis, pages 166-170

23 Robert, pages 490-491

24 Cannon, page 64

25 Riddick, pages 52-53

26 Merriam Webster's *Rules of Order*, page 64

27 Sturgis, *Learning* page 27

28 Riddick, page 207

29 Sturgis, *Learning*, pages 61-62

30 This famous quotation by Winston Churchill may be found in many texts, but its source is a speech to the House of Commons, British Parliament, in November, 1947.

31 Roberta McDow, "What's in a Name?", *Parliamentary Journal*, American Institute of Parliamentarians, XXXI, 1990, page 8.

32 Thomas Jefferson, quoted in *Thomas Jefferson -- Writings,* published by the Library of America (Literary Classics of the United States, Inc., New York, N.Y. 1984.